Biscuiteers Book of Iced Gifts

MICHAEL JOSEPH
an imprint of
PENGUIN BOOKS

Biscuiteers Book
of Iced Gifts

Contents

Our Icing Adventure

Ten years ago, we had a great idea. We decided to launch collections of beautifully iced biscuits in fabulous packaging; a new way of gifting that would be more thoughtful and personal and which would be underpinned by strong design.

From the very beginning, we worked with artists, people who understood the design aesthetic we wanted to create and would enjoy the time and care that goes into making beautiful presents. They were the beginnings of the extraordinary team that has helped us grow and develop the business.

The marvellous thing about biscuits – apart from eating them of course – is their flexibility. They are truly a blank canvas on which to express your creativity. We think that there is absolutely a biscuit for every occasion and have spent the last ten years testing that theory! From the start, our design process has been inspired by life's important milestones and we have enjoyed exploring themes

that underpin our approach to quintessentially British design. Our launch collections included some of our favourites – handbags, bugs and beautiful mummy and baby ducks for new-borns.

Our design process is continuous – we have monthly product development meetings to agree ideas and then our senior biscuit designers start with a mood board, colour palette and icing designs on paper. We look for inspiration from artists, interior design, fashion and current trends. Ultimately, it has to fit our own brand ethos – British, witty – and hang together as a coherent design concept.

Almost as important as the biscuits are the tins. We worked hard to find really beautiful tins, with lovely square-edged corners, which we customise with our own original illustrations that you'll see in this book. We really believe that gifting is an experience to be enjoyed and those finishing touches make all the difference. One of the most rewarding things about creating biscuit gifts is that all your friends

will want to share them – biscuits are real Instagram stars! At Biscuiteers HQ we love hearing our customers' gifting stories and seeing the happiness the biscuits bring to both the recipient and the gifter.

The real heroes of the Biscuiteers story are the icers – the incredible team of dedicated people who use old-fashioned hand-icing techniques to create every single biscuit individually – as hundreds of biscuits became thousands, and then millions. We are proud to have graphic designers, artists and textile designers among our team, as well as cake decorators and bakers. The whole team is trained at Biscuiteers, in all our key icing techniques, which we have shared for you here. Icing takes time, practice and patience, but is hugely rewarding.

The last ten years have been a roller-coaster ride, but have also taken us places we didn't expect and we've created some amazing partnerships along the way. Some of our most exciting projects have been those in which we developed our style of 'biscuit architecture'.

In 2013, we were asked to design Selfridges' main Christmas window, a landscape of 'lost London' (the buildings that no longer exist or were designed and not built). Following this, we have taken on projects to build Charlie's chocolate factory for the West End musical, Leeds Castle and Waddesdon Manor, all entirely in biscuit and icing. Biscuit buildings are challenging, but great fun, and we have included some projects for you to try here.

We also love creating bespoke designs for our corporate clients. We have been lucky enough to work with some of the most iconic international brands, including Christian Dior, Chanel, Burberry and Ralph Lauren. You will also find us in Selfridges, The Savoy, the Royal Botanic Gardens Kew and Fortnum & Mason.

We sell most of our biscuits from our website but, in 2012, we opened our first icing café in Notting Hill. We wanted to create a place where our customers could visit us and learn to ice like a Biscuiteer at our school of icing.

Our customers can also drop in and get creative with biscuits and icing, just like a pottery café. It's the perfect activity for big and little Biscuiteers alike. Our second icing café, on the Northcote Road in South London, opened its doors in 2014.

This book is a collection of some of our favourite projects, and includes some unusual ways to explore the art of gifting with biscuits. You will find recipes, helpful icing guides and, hopefully, masses of inspiration. There is lots more on our blog and social media feeds and, of course, we would love to see you in our icing cafés in London.

Harriet Hastings
Founder and MD of Biscuiteers

www.biscuiteers.com
@biscuiteersltd
#biscuiteering

Key Ingredients and Equipment

Ingredients

Egg white powder (we use Meri-White)

Good-quality plain flour

Good-quality self-raising flour

Granulated and caster sugar

Golden syrup

Salted and unsalted butter

Eggs (large and medium)

Vanilla pods/vanilla extract

Good-quality cocoa powder

Icing sugar

Food colourings (we use gel colours for colouring icing, and paste or powder colours for fondant)

Fondant icing

Marzipan

Edible metallic paints

Lustre dust/shimmer powders

Decorations (sprinkles, golden balls, sanding sugar, hundreds and thousands)

Equipment

Weighing scales (as accurate as possible)

Sieve

Mixing bowls (for mixing biscuit and cake ingredients)

Large smooth rolling pin

Greaseproof paper/baking parchment

Biscuit cutters

Baking trays

Cooling racks

Spatula

Palette knife

Small bowls (for colouring icing)

Piping bags (disposable, reusable plastic or fabric)

Piping nozzles (optional)

Squeezy piping bottles

Toothpicks

Food-safe paintbrush (clean)

20-cm/8-inch cake tins

Pastry brush

String

Fondant cake smoother

25-cm/10-inch cake board

Long wooden skewers or paper lolly sticks (for biscuit pops)

Dough Making and Biscuit Baking

Mastering the art of dough making is the first step in becoming
a Biscuiteer – we've spent ten years perfecting our technique.
Here, you'll find the trusted dough recipes we make every day.
If you have a favourite biscuit recipe of your own, keep in
mind that you need a dough that bakes evenly and is smooth
in texture, to make it easy to ice on.

Top tips for dough making

- Clear a nice big space on your worktop.
- Prepare two baking trays (or more, if you're making a big batch!) with a sheet of greaseproof paper on each.
- Read the recipe from start to finish before you begin.
- Measure all the ingredients before you start. It's also a good idea to test your scales first, to ensure accuracy (use a can of tomatoes or something that has a given weight).
- Take the butter out of the fridge 15 minutes before needed, to come to the right temperature.

Roll with it

We recommend rolling out the dough as soon as it's made, because it's easiest to work with at this time. If you're making a batch to bake later, roll the dough into a disc shape and cover with cling film before chilling. Always bring the dough back to room temperature before attempting to roll out. We roll our dough between two sheets of greaseproof paper, so we don't have to add additional flour that can make the dough dry and less tasty! We also refrigerate our dough for 30 minutes before cutting, so that it handles easier and holds its shape better, even when using the most intricate of cutters!

- Divide the dough in half and shape into two flat discs.
- Place a disc of dough on a sheet of greaseproof paper.
- To roll the dough as evenly as possible, you can use professional rolling guides, or improvise with wooden spoons. Place them either side of the paper to roll directly onto.
- Gently squash the dough down with the rolling pin, then cover with a second sheet of greaseproof paper.
- Begin to roll the dough out with the rolling pin. If the top sheet of paper creases, just peel it off, smooth down and start rolling again.
- Gently roll the dough until it is an even thickness of 5mm all over (or 7mm if you are making biscuit pops).
- Transfer the sheet of rolled dough (still sandwiched between the greaseproof paper) to a baking tray. Place in the fridge to chill for at least 30 minutes before cutting.
- Repeat with the rest of the dough.

Cutting and cooking the dough

- Preheat the oven to 150°C/130°C fan/gas mark 2.

- Line baking trays with greaseproof paper, so you can transfer the biscuits straight over.

- Remove the dough from the fridge just before cutting.

- Assemble your cutters and make a note of how many of each shape you'll need. It's always a good idea to cut a few more than you need, so you're not icing under pressure later on!

- Use the dough efficiently, by cutting the biscuits as close together as possible. Any trimmings can be re-rolled a couple of times.

- After cutting, carefully pick up each biscuit with a palette knife and place onto the lined baking trays. Space the biscuits out evenly – they will spread a little when baking.

- Place the trays into the preheated oven and bake for 20–30 minutes. Check the biscuits after 20 minutes. Bake times vary – large biscuits and large quantities in the oven will take longer.

- When the biscuits are evenly cooked and just beginning to turn a golden colour (vanilla flavour) or darken slightly (chocolate flavour), remove from the oven and transfer the whole sheet of greaseproof paper to a cooling rack. Do this very carefully, as the biscuits will be fragile and hot!

- Cool completely before storing or they will lose their crunch. Don't start to ice the biscuits while they are still warm or the icing will melt off.

- If you are storing to ice later, pack the biscuits between sheets of greaseproof paper in an airtight tin or plastic Tupperware, for up to a week.

Biscuit Recipes

Vanilla Biscuits

This is the classic Biscuiteers recipe – our very first batch of biscuits was a vanilla dough and we've not wavered since. The natural sweetness of vanilla works perfectly with the icing and the light-coloured dough makes it super simple to know when it's cooked.

Makes approx. 24 biscuits

170g caster sugar

170g salted butter

170g golden syrup

1 large egg

1 tsp vanilla extract

480g plain flour

130g self-raising flour

1. Preheat oven to 150°C/130°C fan/gas mark 2. Line two baking trays with greaseproof paper.

2. Put the sugar, butter, golden syrup, egg and vanilla into a large mixing bowl. Mix with an electric mixer on a low speed for 3 minutes, until there are only small lumps of butter visible, then turn the speed of the mixer up to medium for 1 minute to reduce the size of the butter lumps.

3. Sift both types of flour into the bowl and mix on a low speed for 1 minute, or until combined, then turn the mixer up to medium speed for 30 seconds, or until the dough clings together and the sides of the bowl are clean.

4. Turn the dough out onto a clean work surface. Divide into two and squash into even, flat discs. Cover with cling film and chill, or use immediately.

5. Roll out the dough to an even thickness between two sheets of greaseproof paper and cut out your biscuit shapes (for dough rolling, cutting, cooking and keeping tips, see pp.15–16).

6. Carefully pick up each biscuit with a palette knife and place onto the lined trays. Space the biscuits out evenly – they will spread a little when baking.

7. Place the trays into the preheated oven and bake for 20–30 minutes (check at 20 minutes).

8. When the biscuits are evenly cooked and just beginning to turn a golden colour, remove from the oven and transfer the whole sheet of greaseproof paper to a cooling rack. Do this very carefully, as the biscuits will be fragile and hot! Allow to cool completely before icing.

TOP TIP – *If you want to experiment with flavours, the vanilla in this recipe can be replaced with lovely things such as grated lemon or orange zest, coffee or cinnamon. Just keep in mind that you need a dough that bakes evenly and is smooth in texture, so avoid chunky ingredients.*

All-Spice Biscuits

Our all-spice dough started as a Christmas favourite, but now we bake it all year round to make our family of Jolly Gingerbread Men. The all-spice flavours are more subtle than gingerbread, so it's perfect for big and little Biscuiteers alike.

Makes approx. 24 biscuits

170g caster sugar

170g salted butter

170g golden syrup

1 large egg

520g plain flour

80g self-raising flour

1½ tsp mixed spice

1. Preheat oven to 150°C/130°C fan/gas mark 2. Line two baking trays with greaseproof paper.

2. Put the sugar, butter, golden syrup and egg into a large mixing bowl. Mix with an electric mixer on a low speed for 3 minutes, until there are only small lumps of butter visible, then turn the speed of the mixer up to medium for 1 minute to reduce the size of the butter lumps.

3. Sift both types of flour and the mixed spice into the bowl and mix on a low speed for 1 minute, or until combined, then turn the mixer up to medium speed for 30 seconds, or until the dough clings together and the sides of the bowl are clean.

4. Turn the dough out onto a clean work surface. Divide into two and squash into even, flat discs. Cover with cling film and chill, or use immediately.

5. Roll out the dough to an even thickness between two sheets of greaseproof paper and cut out your biscuit shapes (for dough rolling, cutting, cooking and keeping tips, see pp.15–16).

6. Carefully pick up each biscuit with a palette knife and place onto the lined trays. Space the biscuits out evenly – they will spread a little when baking.

7. Place the trays into the preheated oven and bake for 20–30 minutes (check at 20 minutes).

8. When the biscuits are evenly cooked and just beginning to turn golden brown, remove from the oven and transfer the whole sheet of greaseproof paper to a cooling rack. Do this very carefully, as the biscuits will be fragile and hot! Allow to cool completely before icing.

Chocolate Biscuits

It will come as no surprise that chocolate is our customers' favourite, and we bake hundreds of biscuits with this very recipe every day. The rich, chocolatey dough makes the perfect treat for a birthday party or special gift.

Makes approx. 24 biscuits

170g caster sugar

170g salted butter

170g golden syrup

1 large egg

375g plain flour

125g self-raising flour

100g cocoa powder (100%)

1. Preheat oven to 150°C/130°C fan/gas mark 2. Line two baking trays with greaseproof paper.

2. Put the sugar, butter, golden syrup and egg into a large mixing bowl. Mix with an electric mixer on a low speed for 3 minutes, until there are only small lumps of butter visible, then turn the speed up to medium for 1 minute to reduce the size of the butter lumps.

3. Sift both types of flour and the cocoa into the bowl and mix on a low speed for 1 minute, or until combined, then turn the mixer up to medium speed for 30 seconds, or until the dough clings together and the sides of the bowl are clean.

4. Turn the dough out onto a clean work surface. Divide into two and squash into even, flat discs. Cover with cling film and chill, or use immediately.

5. Roll out the dough to an even thickness between two sheets of greaseproof paper and cut out your biscuit shapes (for dough rolling, cutting, cooking and keeping tips, see pp.15–16).

6. Carefully pick up each biscuit with a palette knife and place onto the lined trays. Space the biscuits out evenly – they will spread a little when baking.

7. Place the trays into the preheated oven and bake for 20–30 minutes (check at 20 minutes).

8. When the biscuits are evenly cooked and just beginning to darken slightly, remove from the oven and transfer the whole sheet of greaseproof paper to a cooling rack. Do this very carefully, as the biscuits will be fragile and hot! Allow to cool completely before icing.

Gluten-Free Biscuits

Our customers asked for gluten-free biscuits, so we developed these recipes with many taste tests. It's a hard life! Like us, you'll find them handy to have up your sleeve. Be sure to chill the dough for 1 hour before you start rolling out – it's important not to skip this step.

Vanilla

Makes approx. 24 biscuits

170g caster sugar

170g salted butter

170g golden syrup

1 large egg

1½ tsp vanilla extract

675g gluten-free plain flour
(Doves Farm works well)

½ tsp gluten-free baking powder

1½ tsp xanthan gum

1. Preheat oven to 150°C/130°C fan/gas mark 2. Line two baking trays with greaseproof paper.

2. Put the sugar and butter into a large mixing bowl and mix with an electric mixer, until combined and smooth.

3. Add in the golden syrup and mix until combined.

4. Add in the egg and vanilla and mix on a low speed, until just combined, then turn the speed up to high for about 30 seconds.

5. Sift the gluten-free flour, gluten-free baking powder and xanthan gum into the bowl and mix on a low speed, until combined, then turn the

mixer up to a medium speed for 30 seconds, or until the dough clings together and the sides of the bowl are clean (no more than 1 minute).

6. Turn the dough out onto a clean work surface. Flatten into a disc with the palm of your hand, wrap the dough in cling film and then chill in the fridge for about 1 hour, until firm.

7. Knead the chilled dough until it is very tight, then roll out the dough to an even thickness between two sheets of greaseproof paper. Cut out your biscuit shapes (for dough rolling, cutting, cooking and keeping tips, see pp.15–16).

8. Carefully pick up each biscuit with a palette knife and place onto the lined trays. Space the biscuits out evenly – they will spread a little when baking.

9. Place the trays into the preheated oven and bake for 25–35 minutes (check at 25 minutes).

10. When the biscuits are evenly cooked and just beginning to turn golden, remove from the oven and transfer the whole sheet of greaseproof paper to a cooling rack. Do this very carefully, as the biscuits will be fragile and hot! Allow to cool completely before icing.

Chocolate

Makes approx. 24 biscuits

170g caster sugar

170g salted butter

170g golden syrup

1 large egg

1½ tsp vanilla extract

500g gluten-free plain flour
(Doves Farm works well)

½ tsp gluten-free baking powder

100g cocoa powder (100%)

1½ tsp xanthan gum

1. Preheat oven to 150°C/130°C fan/gas mark 2. Line two baking trays with greaseproof paper.

2. Put the sugar and butter into a large mixing bowl and mix with an electric mixer, until combined and smooth.

3. Add in the golden syrup and mix until combined.

4. Add in the egg and vanilla and mix on a low speed, until just combined, then turn the speed up to high for about 30 seconds.

5. Sift the gluten-free flour, gluten-free baking powder, cocoa powder and xanthan gum into the bowl and mix on a low speed, until combined, then turn the mixer up to a medium speed for 30 seconds, or until the dough clings together and the sides of the bowl are clean (no more than 1 minute).

6. Turn the dough out onto a clean work surface. Flatten into a disc with the palm of your hand, wrap the dough in cling film and then chill in the fridge for about 1 hour, until firm.

7. Knead the chilled dough until it is very tight, then roll out the dough to an even thickness between two sheets of greaseproof paper. Cut out your biscuit shapes (for dough rolling, cutting, cooking and keeping tips, see pp.15–16).

8. Carefully pick up each biscuit with a palette knife and place onto the lined baking trays. Space the biscuits out evenly – they will spread a little when baking.

9. Place the trays into the preheated oven and bake for 25–35 minutes (check at 25 minutes).

10. When the biscuits are evenly cooked and just beginning to darken slightly, remove from the oven and transfer the whole sheet of greaseproof paper to a cooling rack. Do this very carefully, as the biscuits will be fragile and hot! Allow to cool completely before icing.

Cake Recipes

Biscuits may have been our first love, but we think extra-special occasions deserve extra-special cakes. In this chapter, you'll find the cake recipes we use in our bakery. Throughout the book you'll find creative inspiration on how to decorate them (using biscuits, of course!).

Super Chocolatey Cake

Makes 3 x 20-cm/8-inch round cake layers

400g unsalted butter, at room temperature, plus extra for greasing

400g dark chocolate

170g plain flour

170g self-raising flour

½ tsp bicarbonate of soda

400g brown sugar

400g caster sugar

50g cocoa powder (100%)

6 medium eggs, beaten

1. Preheat oven to 160°C/140°C fan/gas mark 3. Grease and line 3 x 20-cm/8-inch round cake tins with greaseproof paper.

2. Place the butter and dark chocolate in a heatproof bowl set over a pan of gently simmering water (make sure the base of the bowl does not touch the water). Use a metal spoon to stir, until completely melted. Set aside to cool a little.

3. Sift together the flours, bicarbonate of soda, sugars and cocoa powder in a large mixing bowl, and stir to combine.

4. Beat the eggs into the chocolate mixture.

5. Pour the chocolate mixture into the dry mixture and stir until combined.

6. Divide the mixture among the prepared tins.

7. Place on the middle shelf of your hot oven and bake for 50 minutes. Check one by inserting a skewer into the middle of the cake. If baked, the skewer will come out clean. If not, pop the cakes back in the oven for 5 minutes more!

8. Allow the cakes to cool in the tins for a few minutes, before turning out onto a wire rack.

Red Velvet Cake

Makes 3 x 20-cm/8-inch round cake layers

180g unsalted butter, at room temperature,
plus extra for greasing

450g caster sugar

2 tsp vanilla extract

3 medium eggs, beaten

450g plain flour

1 tbsp salt

50g dark cocoa powder

360ml buttermilk

1 tbsp red food colouring

1½ tbsp cider vinegar

1½ tsp bicarbonate of soda

1. Preheat oven to 170°C/150°C fan/gas mark 3.
   Grease and line 3 x 20-cm/8-inch round cake tins
   with greaseproof paper.

2. In a large mixing bowl, cream together butter and
   sugar with an electric mixer, until light and fluffy.

3. Scrape down the sides of the mixing bowl, add the
   vanilla, then gradually add the beaten eggs and
   mix together.

4. In a separate large bowl, sift together the flour, salt
   and cocoa powder.

5. Add half of the flour mixture to the batter and
   mix in. Add half of the buttermilk and mix in.
   Repeat with the other halves.

6. Add in the red food colouring and mix well.

7. Mix together the vinegar and bicarbonate of soda,
   then add to the batter and give it a final mix.

8. Divide the mixture among the prepared tins.

9. Bake in the hot oven for 30–35 minutes.
   Check one by inserting a skewer into the middle of
   the cake. If baked, the skewer will come out clean.
   If not, pop the cakes back in the oven for
   5 minutes more!

Zesty Lemon Cake

Makes 3 x 20-cm/8-inch round cake layers

540g unsalted butter, plus extra for greasing

540g caster sugar

8 medium eggs, beaten

25g lemon zest (from about 2 large lemons)

540g self-raising flour

1½ tsp baking powder

1. Preheat oven to 170°C/150°C fan/gas mark 3.
   Grease and line 3 x 20-cm/8-inch round cake tins
   with greaseproof paper.

2. In a large mixing bowl, cream together butter and
   sugar with an electric mixer, until light and fluffy.

3. Scrape down the sides of the mixing bowl,
   then gradually add your beaten eggs and
   mix together. If it looks as though your batter
   is curdling, you can add 1 teaspoon of flour!

4. Fold the lemon zest into the batter.

5. In a separate large bowl, sift together the flour
   and baking powder, then fold into the batter.

6. Divide the mixture among the prepared tins.

7. Bake in the hot oven for 30–35 minutes,
   until golden brown. Check one by inserting a
   skewer into the middle of the cake. If baked,
   the skewer will come out clean. If not, pop the
   cakes back in the oven for 5 minutes more!

Mature Fruit Cake

Makes 1 x 20-cm/8-inch round cake

120g mixed dried fruit

120g chopped apricots

120g chopped dried figs

120g chopped dried dates

120g cranberries

120g mixed peel

120g glacé cherries

150ml Calvados brandy, plus 2 tbsp

200ml hot water

125g unsalted butter, at room temperature

125g dark brown sugar

4 medium eggs

125g wholemeal flour

2 tsp ground nutmeg

6 tsp mixed spice

1 tsp ground cinnamon

1 tsp salt

85g ground almonds

1½ tbsp lemon juice

2 tsp lemon zest

1. Mix all the fruit together in a large mixing bowl and pour over the 150ml brandy and hot water. Leave the fruit to soak at least overnight, or up to a week in advance!

2. Preheat oven to 155°C/135°C fan/gas mark 2.

3. Double-line a heavy duty, 20-cm/8-inch cake tin with greaseproof paper (you need two layers of paper in the tin, as it's a long baking time and you want an even bake!).

4. In a large mixing bowl, cream together the butter and dark brown sugar with an electric mixer, until light and fluffy.

5. Turn the mixer down to a low speed and add in the eggs, one at a time, until all have been incorporated.

6. Fold in the wholemeal flour, spices, salt and ground almonds with a wooden spoon.

7. Then, with your mixer on a low speed, mix in the pre-soaked fruit, lemon juice and zest.

8. Pour the batter into your double-lined cake tin, then cover with foil and place on the middle shelf of the hot oven.

9. Bake for 2 hours, then remove the foil and bake for a further 20 minutes.

10. Remove the cake from the oven and spoon 2 tablespoons of brandy over the cake while it is still warm, letting it soak in.

11. Once cool, wrap your cake in greaseproof paper and cling film, and store in a cool dry place.

TOP TIP – *Your fruit cake can be made 4 months in advance to mature, or used after a couple of weeks.*

Icing Recipes

We use mountains of royal icing every day! We have bowls
and bowls of white, fluffy icing waiting to be hand-coloured
and put into piping bags ready for action. The basic recipe
can be approached three ways. We recommend having a
go at each method and finding the one that suits you best.

Ingredients for royal icing

Powdered egg white recipe

180ml water

1kg icing sugar, sifted

30g egg white powder

All-in-one recipe

150ml cold water

900g royal icing mix

Fresh egg white recipe

4 fresh egg whites (medium)

900g icing sugar, sifted

Combine the ingredients in a mixing bowl, adding
the liquids first – add 100ml water to the bowl to
start with (or most of the fresh egg whites). Add the
dry ingredients and whisk for 5 minutes with an
electric whisk, or for longer with a wooden spoon.
Whisk slowly initially, to avoid clouds of icing sugar!
Continue whisking, gradually adding more water
(or egg white), until you achieve the desired
consistency – a smooth, bright white paste, which
is the thickness of toothpaste (you may need to use
less or more water than the recipe states – go slowly
and judge when you've reached the correct point).

Use immediately, or cover with cling film and chill,
for no longer than 24 hours.

Creating 'line' and 'flood' icings

Once you've mastered royal icing, the next stage is
transforming it into batches of line and flood icing.
Line icing is the consistency of toothpaste and is
used for outlining your biscuits and adding detail.
Flood icing is the consistency of custard and used
to fill larger areas or sections of the biscuit with
a smooth, shiny surface.

As a rule, we allocate two-thirds of the royal icing
mixture to making flood icing; the other third is for
line icing. If you are icing biscuits that require more
of one type or another, adjust accordingly.

Line icing

You don't need to change the consistency of the
royal icing recipe for line icing. Simply look at
how many colour variations you need and divide
up the icing into clean, dry bowls (see p.33 for
colouring technique).

Flood icing

Place the royal icing in a large bowl. Add water,
a few drops at a time, stirring constantly, until you
have a pourable mixture of the same consistency
as custard. Check how many colour variations
you need and divide up into clean, dry bowls
(see p.33 for colouring technique).

Colour Chart

Cream

Purple

Yellow

Lilac

Orange

Pale Green

Red

Lime Green

Hot Pink

Pale Blue

Baby Pink

Blue

Colouring Icing

Once you have your flood and line icing separated into bowls, you can colour them. You should have one bowl for each colour and type of icing, so be sure to check the colourways on the collection you've chosen to ice. You can follow our colourways to a tee, or invent your own. Just be sure to plan thoroughly before you begin, so you don't have to make an emergency batch of icing halfway through! We never start to ice until we have our full set of colours made up, both line and flood.

At Biscuiteers, we use food-colouring gels to create strong and vibrant colours. Traditional bottles of liquid food colouring are okay for paler colours, but for bright and intense colours, we always recommend using food-colouring gels. Most cookshops stock the gels and the internet is an Aladdin's cave for them.

Gel colouring

Use the tip of a cocktail stick to add a tiny amount of gel to the icing. Stir the gel into the icing until it is completely mixed in and you see the resulting colour. Slowly add more gel, stirring well between each addition, until you achieve your desired shade. Cover the surface of the icing with cling film and chill each bowl as you make it, until you have all the colours that you need for the collection.

Bottled liquid food colouring

Using the same method as for gels, drop a little of the liquid food colouring in at a time, stirring intermittently, until you reach the desired shade. You may need to mix in a little extra icing sugar if the liquid colour begins to thin down your line icing.

Natural food colouring

Natural food colouring can be a fantastic alternative to gels or liquid and there are some brilliant websites with handy guides on how to make your own, using ingredients such as matcha, beetroot, turmeric and coffee. At Biscuiteers, we use natural colouring where we can, however, for truly bright and vibrant colours, gels are your best option.

Filling Piping Bags and Bottles

This is the last step before the fun begins! In the Biscuiteers kitchen, we put line icing into piping bags and flood icing into squeezy bottles. Along with the benefits of extra control or quicker coverage, it allows us to immediately tell the difference between the different types of icing, which can be tricky when you're working in the same colour.

Piping bags

We use disposable plastic piping bags. You can cut the tip at an angle to achieve a thin, crisp line and, most importantly, tie them tightly at the top to avoid spillages! Parchment paper cones can also work and are available from most baking shops, or they are easy to make at home with some greaseproof paper.

To fill a piping bag with line icing, place it inside a drinking glass for stability, ensuring that the open end is folded around the lip of the glass. Carefully spoon the icing into the bag, using a flexible spatula to scoop up all the icing from the bowl. When the bag is two-thirds full, pick it up and tie a tight knot at the open end. Holding the knot, carefully swing the bag around a couple of times – this helps gravity push the icing to the tip of the bag! Set aside and start on the next piping bag. Do not cut the tip off the bag until you want to use the colour.

TOP TIP – *It is easier to pipe with less line icing in a bag than more!*

Squeezy bottles

Squeezy bottles are perfect for flood icing – you can sit them flat on a surface while filling and the sturdy nozzles are great for controlling a stream of runny icing onto your biscuit. Lots of different sizes are available, but we recommend the smaller ones for icing at home. To fill a squeezy bottle with flood icing, carefully pour the icing directly from the bowl, using a flexible spatula to guide it through the wide bottle neck. Fasten the lid on tightly and give it a good shake to get rid of air bubbles.

Cake Icings

Vanilla buttercream
Makes enough to ice 1 x 3-layer cake

250g unsalted butter, at room temperature

500g icing sugar, sifted

2 tsp vanilla extract, or the seeds of 1 vanilla pod

1. Put the butter and icing sugar into a large mixing bowl. Use an electric mixer to cream the butter and icing sugar together, until pale and fluffy. This should take about 5 minutes.
2. Add in the vanilla and beat until fully incorporated.

   TOP TIP – *If your buttercream is too thick, add a little milk, 1 teaspoon at a time, until you reach your desired consistency!*

Chocolate buttercream
Makes enough to ice 1 x 3-layer cake

250g unsalted butter, at room temperature

500g icing sugar, sifted

25g cocoa powder (100%), sifted

1. Put the butter and icing sugar into a large mixing bowl. Use an electric mixer to cream the butter and icing sugar together, until pale and fluffy. This should take about 5 minutes.
2. Add in the cocoa powder and beat until fully incorporated.

Cream cheese icing
Makes enough to ice 1 x 3-layer cake

200g unsalted butter, at room temperature

850g icing sugar, sifted

1 tsp vanilla extract

200g cream cheese, at room temperature (the Philadelphia brand works well)

1 tsp cider vinegar

1. Put the butter, icing sugar and vanilla into a large mixing bowl and cream together using an electric mixer, until light and fluffy.
2. Slowly beat in the cream cheese.
3. Finally, mix in the vinegar, until well combined.

Icing Techniques

Note before icing biscuits in this book:

Not every biscuit shown in the photographs has been explained in detail in the method text. Feel free to use the extra biscuits for inspiration. Once you have become familiar with the various icing techniques, you can easily copy them from the photographs, or use them as a starting point to come up with your own unique designs.

How to use line icing

Gently squeeze the icing to the tip of your piping bag. Hold the bag with your writing hand, as you would a pen, and use your other hand to guide as you pipe. Hover the tip of the piping bag just above the biscuit and slowly squeeze the bag with your writing hand, with a consistent pressure. As the icing comes out of the tip and connects with the biscuit, lift the piping bag off the biscuit very slightly and move along to create a line. Stop squeezing just before the point you want to finish and touch the piping bag back onto the surface of the biscuit to break off the line.

How to pipe an outline

The majority of your biscuits will require an outline 'wall' of line icing, to hold the wet flood icing in place. Follow the steps on how to use line icing. The outline on your biscuits should be as close to the outer edge as possible and can have no gaps, otherwise the flood icing will break through and leak down the sides of the biscuit! Outlines should be left to dry at room temperature for 10 minutes before flooding.

How to use flood icing

Using a squeezy bottle filled with flood icing, fill in your outlined biscuits. Start at the outer edges of your biscuit and work your way into the middle using a back-and-forth motion, being careful not to over-fill! After flooding your biscuits, place them onto a lined baking tray and into an oven set to the lowest temperature (50°C/gas mark ¼) for 40 minutes, or until dry. This ensures that the biscuits stay crunchy and you achieve a shiny, smooth icing surface.

When to use line icing on dry flood icing

Line icing is also used for adding detail. Once the flood icing on your biscuits is completely dry, outline the flooded sections with line icing to make them look sharper. Most of the collections call for line icing on top on flood icing to create detail and designs.

Flood-on-flood

Immediately after flooding your biscuits, while the icing is still wet, you can pipe details of contrasting flood icing directly into the wet base. We find that some of the most effective (and simple!) flood-on-flood techniques are stripes and polka dots. You must not over-fill the biscuit on the initial flood, otherwise you will find that the icing will spill over the edges when more is added.

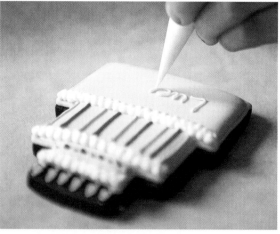

Feathering

Flood the biscuit with different coloured lines of flood icing. While the icing is still wet, take a cocktail stick and lightly drag it through the lines of icing to create a feather pattern. You can do this in alternating directions. Wipe the cocktail stick clean in between each drag. It's important to do this while the icing is still wet, so that the pattern 'sinks in' and you achieve a smooth surface when dry.

Writing with line icing

Cut a very fine hole with scissors at the end of your piping bag. Hold your piping bag like a pen and follow the instructions on p.37 on how to use line icing.

TOP TIP – *Before piping directly onto your biscuit, we recommend first writing out the word/s you want to pipe with a pencil or pen onto greaseproof paper. Then, practice following the lines with your piping bag – it is always good to have a practice first!*

Using hundreds and thousands and sanding sugar

While the flood icing on your biscuit is still wet (either the whole base or just a section that you want to cover), use a spoon to sprinkle your hundreds and thousands or sanding sugar directly onto the wet area. Start with a little and add more as necessary. Leave for a couple of minutes to dry, then gently tap off any excess.

Edible balls and decorations

Using line icing, pipe a small dot onto your biscuit wherever you wish to attach your decoration – this will act as glue. While the dot of icing is still wet, gently press your ball or decoration into the wet icing and hold for a few seconds. Then set to one side and leave to fully dry for 10 minutes.

Lustre dusts and shimmers

Lustre dusts and shimmers are great for adding extra sparkle to cakes and biscuits. Take a clean, food-safe paintbrush, dip it into your shimmer and brush a thin layer directly onto dry icing or a fondant-covered cake.

Edible metallic paints

Edible metallic paints are perfect for achieving a pearlescent or metallic look. Once your biscuits are completely dry, use a clean, food-safe paintbrush, dip it into edible metallic paint, then brush directly onto your biscuits. A little bit goes a long way, so start off sparingly. Leave to dry at room temperature for 5–10 minutes.

Gift Wrapping Ideas

Hand-iced biscuits make the perfect gift, as they are a completely unique and thoughtful way to celebrate special occasions. They are not only witty and stylish, but their incredible flexibility means that you can create a biscuit collection for every occasion and post them to your friends and family, all over the world.

At Biscuiteers, we pack our biscuit collections into square-edged, rectangular tins that feature stunning, original illustrations that correspond to the biscuits inside. From cats, to bugs, to birthday cakes, to babygrows, the illustrations on the tins make the present extra-special and unique to the occasion. The tins protect the delicate biscuits during their journey through the postal system, and make a wonderful keep-sake for the lucky recipient once all the biscuits have been eaten.

We also use sturdy gift boxes that are hand-illustrated with our iconic Notting Hill shop front, into which we pack three or four delicious biscuits. We name these our 'biscuit cards', because they are designed to be posted right through the letterbox, making them a perfectly sweet alternative to the usual birthday or thank-you card.

If you're planning to post your iced biscuits, you'll need to package them up to survive the journey. We ice a tiny spot of line icing on the back of our biscuits to secure them onto a spongy cardboard, called glassine, before layering them inside the tin. Wrapping each biscuit in a cellophane bag and placing into a box full of brightly coloured tissue paper also works. Whatever you choose, be sure that the biscuits only come into contact with packaging that is food-safe and clean.

In our icing cafés, we place our biscuit tins and boxes into a beautiful gift bag, attach a gift tag and tie with a ribbon, ready to be given to your loved one on their special day. If you're hand-delivering your biscuits, there are lots of creative ways to gift wrap or present your creations:

Organza or cellophane bags

Perfect for wedding favours or place settings. Tie with a ribbon that matches the bridal colour-scheme.

Handmade envelopes

Pick your favourite wrapping paper, wallpaper or magazine and simply fold into an envelope.

Handmade Christmas crackers

A great crafty project – take the cardboard interior of a toilet roll and pop a biscuit, a hand-written joke or love note and a snapper inside, before rolling it in Christmas wrapping paper and tying each end with ribbon.

Vintage sweet bags

We love bags with stripes and polka dots for a delightful clash with our brightly coloured biscuit designs. Great for party bags!

Kilner jars

Stack lots of mini-biscuits inside and tie with a ribbon, or stand longer biscuits up inside the jar. We love giving a jar of pencil biscuits to our children's teachers at the end of term.

Reclaimed boxes

Kitchen matchboxes, chocolate boxes or jewellery boxes are all perfect for biscuits. You can re-cover the boxes with your favourite wrapping paper or simply tie with a ribbon. Make sure matchboxes are properly lined, so that they are food-safe.

In the Garden

Climb into your wellies and harvest a bounty of hand-iced veggies – the tastiest way to get your five a day! We love the vibrant colours in this collection and love gifting it to our green-fingered friends even more.

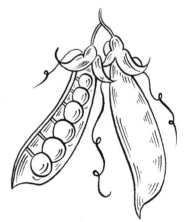

You will need:

1 batch of shaped biscuits (recipes pp.19–25)

1 batch of Royal Icing (recipe p.30), divided into line and flood consistencies (colours detailed in individual biscuit instructions)

Edible silver metallic paint (for the watering can)

Peas in a pod

Line: dark green / white
Flood: bright green

1. Using dark green line icing, outline the shape of the pod on the biscuit. Leave to dry for 10 minutes at room temperature.

2. Once dry, flood the shape with bright green flood icing.

3. Place the biscuit onto a baking tray and into an oven set to the lowest temperature (50°C/gas mark ¼) for 40 minutes, or until the icing has set hard.

4. Use green line icing to pipe a few leaves, a line to divide the pod, and 4 small peas on each side of the line, joining them to the line with a small dot of green line icing. Leave to dry for 5 minutes, then add small 'shine' details to the peas with white line icing. Allow to fully dry.

Tomato

Line: red / dark green
Flood: red

1. Using red line icing, pipe a simple circle shape on the biscuit. Leave to dry for 10 minutes at room temperature.

2. Flood the shape with red flood icing – don't over-fill.

3. Place the biscuit onto a baking tray and into an oven set to the lowest temperature (50°C/gas mark ¼) for 40 minutes, or until the icing has set hard.

4. To finish, use green line icing to add some leaves in a rough 5-point-star shape. Allow to fully dry.

Aubergine

Line: dark purple / dark green
Flood: dark purple / lilac / white

1. Using dark purple line icing, pipe an aubergine shape on your biscuit – it should look a bit like a long kidney bean. Leave to dry for 10 minutes at room temperature.

2. Once dry, use dark purple flood icing to fill in the shape – don't over-fill. While the icing is still wet, pipe 2 lines of lilac flood icing down one side, then a line of white flood in between, letting the icing 'melt' in a little. This creates a 'shiny' effect.

3. Place the biscuit onto a baking tray and into an oven set to the lowest temperature (50°C/gas mark ¼) for 40 minutes, or until the icing has set hard.

4. Use green line icing to pipe a stalk at the top and 5 little lines for leaves. Allow to fully dry.

Watering can

Line: grey
Flood: grey

1. Using grey line icing, pipe the outline of the can, spout and handles. Leave to dry for 10 minutes at room temperature.

2. Once dry, flood the shape with grey flood icing.

3. Place the biscuit onto a baking tray and into an oven set to the lowest temperature (50°C/gas mark ¼) for 40 minutes, or until the icing has set hard.

4. Using grey line icing, pipe details on top to define the spout, rim and handle and leave to dry for 5 minutes.

5. Dip a clean, dry paintbrush into the edible silver metallic paint, then brush over the top of the biscuit. A little goes a long way so use sparingly. Leave to dry for 5–10 minutes.

Bouquet Collection

Mother Nature has long been a muse for us – floral designs are our speciality. We often ask: 'Why send flowers when you can send biscuits instead?' This collection is packed with impressive icing techniques and the vibrant colours are ideal for biscuit icing.

You will need:

1 batch of round biscuits (recipes pp.19–25)

Wooden skewers (to be used during baking – see below)

1 batch of Royal Icing (recipe p.30), divided into line and flood consistencies (colours detailed in individual biscuit instructions)

For biscuit pops:

Make your biscuit dough according to the recipe, but roll it out to a thickness of 7mm. Cut into desired shapes. Before baking (see pp.15–16), carefully thread wooden skewers through the centre of the shapes, taking care not to break the surface of the dough. Bake as usual.

Pansy

Line: purple / yellow / white
Flood: purple / lilac / yellow / hot pink

1. Pipe the outline of your pansy on the biscuit with purple line icing. Make sure you nip in to define each petal, but do not bring the line down into the centre of the shape. Leave to dry for 10 minutes at room temperature.

2. Once dry, flood the outer edge of the flower with purple flood icing. Randomly fill in the rest of the area with lilac, yellow and hot pink flood. Use a cocktail stick to drag the colours into each other – this is called 'feathering'.

3. Place the biscuit onto a baking tray and into an oven set to the lowest temperature (50°C/gas mark ¼) for 40 minutes, or until the icing has set hard.

4. Use purple line icing to pipe around the flower edge and into the centre to create petals. Use yellow line icing to create the middle of your flower, finishing with a dot of white right in the centre. Allow to fully dry.

TOP TIP – *You can also try icing these in reverse colourways!*

Sunflower

Line: yellow / brown
Flood: yellow

1. Using yellow line icing, pipe the outline of a sunflower on the biscuit, rather like a sun, then pipe a small circle in the centre. Leave to dry for 10 minutes at room temperature.

2. Once dry, flood the shape with yellow flood icing.

3. Place the biscuit onto a baking tray and into an oven set to the lowest temperature (50°C/gas mark ¼) for 40 minutes, or until the icing has set hard.

4. Using yellow line icing, pipe small petals all around the flower.

5. Finally, using brown line icing, pipe small dots in the centre of your biscuit, to create the sunflower's seeds. Allow to fully dry.

Peony

Line: white
Flood: white / hot pink

1. Using white line icing, pipe the outline of a peony on the biscuit (nip in slightly to define 4 main petal shapes). Leave to dry for 10 minutes at room temperature.

2. Once dry, flood the shape with randomly placed areas of white and hot pink flood icing. Use a cocktail stick to swirl the two colours round in a circular motion – you want to create a marbled effect.

3. Place the biscuit onto a baking tray and into an oven set to the lowest temperature (50°C/gas mark ¼) for 40 minutes, or until the icing has set hard.

4. Using white line icing, pipe ruffled petals (follow the photograph – it's easiest to work from the centre outwards). Allow to fully dry.

Botanical Bouquet Cake

Mary, Mary, quite contrary, how does your garden grow?
With lots of icing sugar and piping bags, that's how! Our
floral-inspired show-stopper is perfect for a special birthday
or a summer family get-together. You could even add tiers
to create the most beautiful midsummer-wedding cake.

You will need:

3 x 20-cm/8-inch Zesty Lemon Cake layers (recipe p.28)
1 batch of Vanilla Buttercream (recipe p.35)
25-cm/10-inch cake board
Icing sugar, for dusting
1kg fondant icing (shop-bought, at room temperature)
Green food colouring (paste or powder is best for fondant)
1 batch of Royal Icing (recipe p.30), coloured green
Flower biscuit pops (Bouquet Collection biscuits p.49)

1. Bake your cakes according to the recipe. Once the layers
are completely cool, you can stack them up. Using a sharp
knife, carefully level the top of each layer so they sit flat.

2. Smear a little buttercream onto the cake board and place
the first cake layer on top, to secure it to the board.

3. Using a palette knife, spread the buttercream evenly over
the top of the first layer, then place another cake layer
on top. Repeat.

4. Take a generous amount of buttercream and smooth it
around the edge and top of the cake, using a palette knife
or plastic side scraper to scrape off the excess, until the
cake is evenly covered in buttercream.

5. Place the iced cake in the fridge for 30 minutes to firm up.

6. Measure across the top and sides of the cake with a piece
of string or cotton – this will act as a guide for rolling
out your fondant. Cut to size and set aside.

7. Clear a large, smooth work surface so that it is clean and
free of crumbs – imperfections will be visible on your
fondant. Dust the surface generously with icing sugar.

8. Knead the fondant for 2 minutes, or until softened.

9. If you are going to colour your fondant, this is the point to
do it. We coloured ours green. Knead the colour in well
(following the instructions on your packet).

10. Roll the fondant into a ball, then flatten it into a disc.
In order to keep your fondant icing as smooth as possible,
remove all jewellery before you roll out your fondant,
as rings or bracelets could leave marks in the icing!

11. Lightly dust a rolling pin with icing sugar. Roll out the
fondant until it is about 5mm thick, giving it a quarter
turn every now and then, to help keep it even and round.
Use your measured string for guidance – the fondant
should be slightly bigger than the string. Remember,
you can always trim excess fondant later.

12. Loosely drape the fondant over your rolling pin, then lift
and roll it up and over the cake.

13. Smooth the fondant over the cake with a fondant smoother
or a smooth glass. Start on the top of the cake and then
smooth down the sides. Be careful to avoid folds, wrinkles
and air bubbles in the icing.

14. Once the fondant is smooth, use a small knife or pizza
cutter to cut away excess icing at the bottom of the cake.
Try to cut as close to the bottom of the cake as possible.

15. Using green line icing and starting at the bottom of the
cake, pipe spiralling vines upwards all the way onto the top
of the cake. Pipe little leaves at intervals along the vines
and a line of grass at the bottom of the cake. Allow to dry.

16. Now for the fun bit! Insert your flower pops so that it gives
the illusion of flowers growing out of the top of the cake.
Trim the end of your pops with scissors so the flowers stand
at different heights.

OPTIONAL EXTRA – *Tiny leaf biscuits add extra detail to
the cake. Use a small tear-drop cutter to create the biscuits and ice
them using the standard line and flood technique. Pipe a small amount
of line icing onto the back of each biscuit, then carefully stick them to
the side of the cake next to the vines. Leave the icing to dry for about
30 minutes, then it is ready to go!*

Flower-Pot Cake

This witty flower-pot cake is made entirely with sponge and buttercream and is topped with biscuits from our iconic Flower Power Collection. It's guaranteed to raise a smile from every party guest.

You will need:

3 x 20-cm/8-inch Super Chocolatey Cake layers (recipe p.26)

1 batch of Vanilla Buttercream (recipe p.35)

1 batch of Chocolate Buttercream (recipe p.35)

Light brown food colouring

25-cm/10-inch cake board

1 batch of chocolate biscuits (recipe p.23)

Iced flower and leaf biscuits (see instructions opposite for icing Flower Power Collection biscuits, or use Bouquet Collection biscuits p.49)

1. Bake your cakes according to the recipe. While the cakes are cooling, colour the vanilla buttercream with a small amount of the brown food colouring, mixing it in with a metal spoon – you want to create the colour of a plant pot.

   TOP TIP – *Add food colouring just a little bit at a time, building up the colour slowly. Use a cocktail stick to add small amounts of colour to the buttercream, mixing in well before the next addition.*

2. Once the cake layers are completely cool, you can begin to stack them up. Using a sharp knife, carefully level the top of each layer – they will need to sit flat.

3. Smear a little chocolate buttercream in the middle of the cake board. Place the first cake layer on top, securing it to the board.

4. Using a palette knife, spread the chocolate buttercream evenly over the top of the first layer, then place another cake layer on top. Repeat, finishing with a layer of chocolate buttercream on the very top of the cake.

5. Using a sharp knife, shape the cake – it should be wide at the top and taper to the base. Leaving the top layer untrimmed (that will be the lip of the pot), begin trimming the bottom 2 layers evenly downwards to create the shape of a flower pot.

6. Using a palette knife, smooth the coloured vanilla buttercream around the sides of the cake until it is completely covered.

   TOP TIP – *Use a palette knife that you have run under warm water to smooth the buttercream, the warm knife will you give you an extra-smooth and professional finish!*

7. Take the un-iced chocolate biscuits and finely crumble them up on top of the cake, to give the effect of soil. Then finish off the cake with some beautiful iced biscuits in the shape of leaves and flowers.

For the Flower Power Collection

Using the following selection of line and flood icing colours, and copying the designs in the picture, ice a colourful collection of flowers and leaves, remembering to allow the line icing outlines to dry for 10 minutes before the addition of flood icing. Place the biscuits onto a baking tray and into an oven set to the lowest temperature (50°C/gas mark ¼) for 40 minutes, or until the icing has set hard. Add pretty details with line icing and allow to fully dry for 10 minutes before adding to your cake.

Line: green / orange / yellow / raspberry pink / white / violet / turquoise

Flood: green / orange / yellow / raspberry pink / white / violet

Ice Cream Toppers

As soon as the sun makes an appearance, our icing cafés have people queuing around the block for our famous biscuit-topped ice creams. You can be really creative with these, either matching the ice cream flavour to the biscuit design or choosing a theme to complement your event – a whole new approach to the classic 99!

You will need:

1 batch of shaped biscuits (recipes pp. 19–25)

1 batch of Royal Icing (recipe p.30), line icing consistency (colours detailed in individual biscuit instructions)

Sunglasses

Line: light pink / white

1. Use light pink line icing to pipe a frame shape on the biscuit. Use the shape of the glasses in the photograph as a guide and be careful not to pipe over where the lenses would be.

2. Allow to dry at room temperature for 10 minutes, then pipe small dots of white line icing on top for a polka dot effect. Allow to fully dry.

Strawberry

Line: red / yellow / green

1. Using red line icing, pipe a strawberry shape on the biscuit and continue piping in a swirl until you reach the middle.

2. Pipe small dots of yellow line icing on top for the seeds.

3. Finally, pipe 3 green lines at the top for the leaves. Allow to dry at room temperature for about 10 minutes.

Raspberry

Line: hot pink

1. This one is very easy to ice. Using hot pink line icing, pipe a row of dots across the top of the biscuit.

2. Continue in this way around the whole shape, starting from the bottom, adding dots until you reach near the top. Stop just short of the top line. Allow to dry at room temperature for about 10 minutes.

Bee

Line: yellow / black / white

1. Using yellow line icing, begin by piping an oval shape in the middle of the biscuit.

2. Then pipe 2 or 3 thick stripes across the oval in black line icing, with 2 small lines at the top for the antennae.

3. Use white line icing to pipe 2 wings on either side. Pipe these as if you were trying to draw the outline of a leaf. Allow to dry at room temperature for about 10 minutes.

Stackable Burger Biscuits

What could be more fun than a stackable burger made of biscuits?! Personalise the bun with your guests' names to use as place settings, and invite them to create their ideal BBQ treat. Perfect for big and little kids alike.

You will need:

1 batch of shaped biscuits (recipes pp.19–25)

1 batch of Royal Icing (recipe p.30), divided into line and flood consistencies (colours detailed in individual biscuit instructions)

Burger bun

Line: light brown / white
Flood: light brown

1. You'll need two circular biscuits for this, one for the top and one for the bottom of your bun.

2. Using light brown line icing, pipe a circle outline on each biscuit. Leave to dry for 10 minutes at room temperature.

3. Once dry, flood with light brown flood icing.

4. Place the biscuits onto a baking tray and into an oven set to the lowest temperature (50°C/gas mark ¼) for 40 minutes, or until the icing has set hard.

5. Use white line icing to pipe dots onto one of the biscuits to create a sesame-seed effect. Allow to fully dry.

Tomato slice

Line: red / light red / brown
Flood: red

1. Using red line icing, pipe the outline of your tomato on the biscuit. Leave to dry for 10 minutes at room temperature.

2. Once dry, flood with red flood icing.

3. Place the biscuit onto a baking tray and into an oven set to the lowest temperature (50°C/gas mark ¼) for 40 minutes, or until the icing has set hard.

4. Pipe the triangular segments of the tomato with light red line icing and the seeds with brown. Allow to fully dry.

Cheese slice

Line: yellow
Flood: yellow

1. Pipe the outline of your cheese square on the biscuit with yellow line icing, then pipe random circles inside, to create the look of holes in the cheese slice. (You can cut holes in the biscuit before baking if you wish, or just leave the biscuit whole). Leave to dry for 10 minutes.

2. Once dry, flood the shape (but not the centre of the circles) with yellow flood icing.

3. Place the biscuit onto a baking tray and into an oven set to the lowest temperature (50°C/gas mark ¼) for 40 minutes, or until the icing has set hard.

Lettuce

Line: lime green / white
Flood: light green

1. Using lime green line icing, pipe the outline of your lettuce leaf on the biscuit. Leave to dry for 10 minutes.

2. Once dry, flood the shape with light green flood icing.

3. Place the biscuit onto a baking tray and into an oven set to the lowest temperature (50°C/gas mark ¼) for 40 minutes, or until the icing has set hard.

4. Add detail to the biscuit by icing small wiggly lines in white line icing, all over. Allow to fully dry.

Ice Lollies

Introducing our ice-lolly biscuits – a delightful dose of nostalgia and British summertime in one colourful collection. These make fantastic party favours, birthday gifts or end-of-term treats. But be warned, there'll be arguments over which is best, Fab or Twister!

You will need:

1 batch of shaped biscuits (recipes pp.19–25)

1 batch of Royal Icing (recipe p.30), divided into line and flood consistencies (colours detailed in individual biscuit instructions)

Hundreds and thousands sprinkles

Fab ice lolly

Line: white / beige
Flood: brown / red / white / beige

1. Outline the rectangle shape of the lolly with white line icing, then pipe 2 horizontal lines across the biscuit to create 3 sections. Outline the lolly stick at the bottom with beige line icing. Leave to dry for 10 minutes at room temperature.

2. Once dry, flood the top section with brown icing, then, using a spoon, sprinkle your hundreds and thousands over the area and carefully tap off the excess. Leave to dry for 5 minutes.

3. Flood the middle section with white flood icing, the bottom section with red flood icing and the stick with beige flood icing.

4. Place the biscuit onto a baking tray and into an oven set to the lowest temperature (50°C/gas mark ¼) for 40 minutes, or until the icing has set hard.

Rocket ice lolly

Line: yellow / beige / orange
Flood: beige / yellow / orange / red

1. Using yellow line icing, pipe around the shape of the biscuit to create the lolly outline, then pipe 2 horizontal lines across the biscuit to create the segments. Outline the lolly stick at the bottom with beige line icing. Leave to dry for 10 minutes at room temperature.

2. Once dry, flood the stick area with beige flood icing, the bottom section of the lolly with yellow flood, the middle with orange and the top with red. Be careful not to over-fill.

3. Place the biscuit onto a baking tray and into an oven set to the lowest temperature (50°C/gas mark ¼) for 40 minutes, or until the icing has set hard.

4. Pipe 2 vertical lines down the centre of the lolly with orange line icing, then add another 2 on either side, following the shape of the lolly outline. Allow to fully dry.

Twister ice lolly

Line: white / beige / lime green
Flood: white / lime green / bright pink / beige

1. Using white line icing, pipe the outline of your lolly on the biscuit – the edges should be scalloped. Pipe an oval shape at the top, then pipe curved horizontal lines, to create equally sized sections down the lolly.

2. With beige line icing, outline the stick of the lolly at the bottom. Leave to dry for 10 minutes at room temperature.

3. Once dry, use white flood icing to fill the oval shape at the top, and then flood alternate segments with white flood and lime green flood icing.

4. Drop a small amount of bright-pink flood icing into the centre of the top oval section.

5. Flood the stick area with beige flood icing.

6. Place the biscuit onto a baking tray and into an oven set to the lowest temperature (50°C/gas mark ¼) for 40 minutes, or until the icing has set hard.

7. To give your twister lolly some definition, pipe a line of white and lime green line icing at the bottom of each segment to define the sections. Allow to fully dry.

Tropical Fish

If you're dreaming of sun-soaked beaches, white sand, boat rides and snorkelling, our tropical fish collection will take you there! Dive into the Biscuiteers ocean and create your own school of brightly coloured fish.

You will need:

1 batch of shaped biscuits (recipes pp.19–25)

1 batch of Royal Icing (recipe p.30), divided into line and flood consistencies (colours detailed in individual biscuit instructions)

Jellyfish

Line: orange / yellow / white
Flood: orange / yellow

1. Use orange line icing to outline the main body of the jellyfish at the top of the biscuit – you want a domed top and scalloped bottom. Then use yellow line icing to pipe the outline of the rest of the body – scalloped at the top and tapering into a triangle shape (this will be partly hidden by tentacles later!). Leave to dry for 10 minutes at room temperature.

2. Once dry, use orange flood icing to fill in the top shape, and yellow flood to fill in the bottom.

3. Place the biscuit onto a baking tray and into an oven set to the lowest temperature (50°C/gas mark ¼) for 40 minutes, or until the icing has set hard.

4. Using orange line icing, pipe wiggly lines for tentacles coming down from the main body and over the yellow section, and pipe up from the corner of each scalloped edge to create definition on the body.

5. Use white line icing to outline the edge of the top of the dome, then pipe small semi-circles to add definition to each scalloped edge. Allow to fully dry.

Black, white and yellow fish *(top right)*

Line: white / black / yellow
Flood: white / black

1. Pipe around the main body of the fish with white line icing, then outline the fish tail with black line icing.

2. Using white line icing, pipe 4–5 vertical lines down

the fish's body. Leave to dry for 10 minutes at room temperature.

3. Once dry, flood the sections on the body, alternating with white and black flood icing. Flood the tail with black.

4. Place the biscuit onto a baking tray and into an oven set to the lowest temperature (50°C/gas mark ¼) for 40 minutes, or until the icing has set hard.

5. Add detail to the sections and outline the edge of the tail with yellow line icing. Pipe a triangle of black line icing onto the nose of the fish and fill it in with yellow line icing. Use white to pipe a small circle for the eye, then pipe a dot of black directly on top, then a final dot of white on top again. Allow to fully dry.

Blue and orange fish *(far left)*

Line: blue / white / orange / black
Flood: blue / orange

1. Use blue line icing to pipe the outline of your fish on the biscuit. Leave to dry for 10 minutes at room temperature.

2. Once dry, use blue flood icing to fill in the shape.

3. While the icing is still wet, take orange flood icing and pipe lots of lines into the blue to create the patterns on the fish.

4. Place the biscuit onto a baking tray and into an oven set to the lowest temperature (50°C/gas mark ¼) for 40 minutes, or until the icing has set hard.

5. Now give your fish some detail: with blue line icing, pipe small lines to create the shape of a fin in the centre of the fish. Then, around the bottom and top edge, pipe lots of small lines to add texture.

6. Use white line icing to add small dots and lines to the edge of the fish, and outline a mouth shape with orange line icing.

7. Finish with a blob of black line icing for the eye, with a white dot on top. Allow to fully dry.

Autumn Woodland Cake

If you go down to the woods today… Mix the
icing colours for our Woodland Collection (on p.68)
and you'll be transported to misty autumn, with the
low-shining sun and crunchy leaves underfoot.
We've used the biscuits to decorate a luxurious
chocolate cake, but they are equally lovely used
in party bags for autumn birthdays.

You will need:

3 x 20-cm/8-inch Super Chocolatey Cake layers
(recipe p.26)

2 batches of Chocolate Buttercream (recipe p.35)

25-cm/10-inch cake board

1 batch of Vanilla Biscuits (recipe p.19), to decorate

Icing sugar, to decorate (optional)

Woodland Collection biscuits (p.68), to decorate

1. Bake your cakes according to the recipe. Once the
   layers are completely cool, you can stack them up.
   Using a sharp knife, carefully level the top of each cake
   layer so they sit flat.

2. Smear a little buttercream onto the cake board and place
   the first cake layer on top, to secure it to the board.

3. Using a palette knife, spread the buttercream evenly over
   the top of the first layer, then place another cake layer
   on top. Repeat.

4. Take a generous amount of buttercream and smooth it
   around the edge and top of the cake using a palette knife,
   scraping off the excess, until the cake is evenly covered
   in buttercream.

5. Use a palette knife or the back of a spoon to roughen the
   surface of the buttercream – you want to create the effect
   of bark on a tree stump.

6. Crumble some plain vanilla biscuits on top of the cake
   for a mossy effect. You can also sprinkle icing sugar over
   the cake to look like frost, if you like. Finally, decorate
   with your woodland biscuits.

Woodland Collection

You will need:

1 batch of shaped biscuits (recipes pp.19–25)

1 batch of Royal Icing (recipe p.30), divided into line and flood consistencies (colours detailed in individual biscuit instructions)

Rabbit

Line: brown / white
Flood: light brown

1. Using brown line icing, pipe the outline of the body of the rabbit on the biscuit (leave space for the tail, which you will add later). Leave to dry for 10 minutes at room temperature.

2. Once dry, flood the shape with light brown flood icing.

3. Place the biscuit onto a baking tray and into an oven set to the lowest temperature (50°C/gas mark ¼) for 40 minutes, or until the icing has set hard.

4. Add a small dot of brown line icing for an eye, and pipe an even smaller white dot for the centre of the eye.

5. Pipe a small white line to define the rabbit's throat, then pipe small lines back and forth to create a tail. Randomly add a few dots under the tail and on the front legs.

6. Finish off with a small dot of brown line icing for a nose. Allow to fully dry.

Leaf

Line: yellow / red / orange / brown
Flood: yellow / red / orange

1. Using yellow/red/orange line icing, pipe the outline of a leaf on the biscuit. Leave to dry for 10 minutes at room temperature.

2. Once dry, flood the shape with yellow, red or orange flood icing.

3. Place the biscuit onto a baking tray and into an oven set to the lowest temperature (50°C/gas mark ¼) for 40 minutes, or until the icing has set hard.

4. Use brown line icing to pipe the veins of the leaves. Allow to fully dry.

TOP TIP – *You can also try icing these in reverse colours!*

Toadstool

Line: red / white
Flood: red / white

1. Using red line icing, pipe the outline of the top of the toadstool, leaving a section at the bottom for gills, then outline the stalk and gill segment using white line icing. Leave to dry for 10 minutes at room temperature.

2. Once dry, flood the top of the toadstool with red flood icing, then the gill segment and stalk with white flood icing.

3. Place the biscuit onto a baking tray and into an oven set to the lowest temperature (50°C/gas mark ¼) for 40 minutes, or until the icing has set hard.

4. Using white line icing add a spread of dots to the red section. Outline the stalk and create gills with a row of lines at the top and bottom. Allow to fully dry.

Rainy Days

At Biscuiteers we're inspired by all things quintessentially British – and what could be more British than a soggy wet afternoon? We've kept calm and created this ode to our beloved weather – a tongue-in-cheek way to say thank you for that 'summer' holiday with the family!

You will need:

1 batch of shaped biscuits (recipes pp.19–25)

1 batch of Royal Icing (recipe p.30), divided into line and flood consistencies (colours detailed in individual biscuit instructions)

Rain coat

Line: yellow / blue / cream / brown
Flood: yellow / blue

1. Using yellow line icing, outline the shape of your coat on the biscuit, making sure you define a space for the inside of the hood. Leave to dry for 10 minutes at room temperature.

2. Once dry, flood the coat shape with yellow flood icing, and the inside of the hood with blue flood icing.

3. Place the biscuit onto a baking tray and into an oven set to the lowest temperature (50°C/gas mark ¼) for 40 minutes, or until the icing has set hard.

4. Use yellow line icing to define the arms, pockets and hood. Add definition to the hood with a line of blue line icing.

5. Finish off by using cream and brown line icing to create buttons and toggles. Allow to fully dry.

Cloud

Line: white
Flood: white

1. Outline the cloud shape on the biscuit with white line icing. Leave to dry for 10 minutes at room temperature.

2. Once dry, flood the shape with white flood icing.

3. Place the biscuit onto a baking tray and into an oven set to the lowest temperature (50°C/gas mark ¼) for 40 minutes, or until the icing has set hard.

4. Pipe wiggly semi-circles across the biscuit and around the edges with white line icing, to make the cloud look fluffy. Allow to fully dry.

Umbrella

Line: white / grey / pink
Flood: red / hot pink / lime green / orange / purple

1. Outline the umbrella shape on the biscuit using white line icing (don't forget to make sections). Add a handle with grey line icing. Leave to dry for 10 minutes at room temperature.

2. Once dry, flood the middle sections with different bright colours of flood icing.

3. Place the biscuit onto a baking tray and into an oven set to the lowest temperature (50°C/gas mark ¼) for 40 minutes, or until the icing has set hard.

4. Go over the umbrella with white line icing to add definition to the panels.

5. Use pink line icing to define a curved handle at the bottom. At the top of the umbrella add a little pink triangle to finish it off. Allow to fully dry.

Raindrop

Line: shades of blue / white
Flood: shades of blue

1. Outline the raindrop shape on the biscuit using blue line icing. Leave to dry for 10 minutes at room temperature.

2. Once dry, flood the raindrop with blue flood icing.

3. Place the biscuit onto a baking tray and into an oven set to the lowest temperature (50°C/gas mark ¼) for 40 minutes, or until the icing has set hard.

4. Using white line icing, add a dot near the top, then follow the curve of the raindrop along the bottom to add definition. Allow to fully dry.

Breakfast in Bed

Tah dah … introducing the Biscuiteers recipe for the ultimate fry up, complete with a mug of tea to warm up those chilly mornings! We all know someone who deserves breakfast in bed, and we can't think of a sweeter way to treat them.

You will need:

1 batch of shaped biscuits (recipes pp.19–25)

1 batch of Royal Icing (recipe p.30), divided into line and flood consistencies (colours detailed in individual biscuit instructions)

Eggs

Line: white / yellow
Flood: white / yellow

1. Using white line icing, pipe a splatter shape on the biscuit. Leave to dry for 10 minutes at room temperature.

2. Once dry, flood the shape with white flood icing.

3. Place the biscuit onto a baking tray and into an oven set to the lowest temperature (50°C/gas mark ¼) for 40 minutes, or until the icing has set hard.

4. Use yellow line icing to pipe a large circle for the yolk. Dry for 10 minutes, then flood the circle with yellow flood icing. Return to the oven for 30–40 minutes to fully dry.

Toast

Line: beige
Flood: beige / cream

1. Using beige line icing, pipe a toast outline on the biscuit. Leave to dry for 10 minutes at room temperature.

2. Once dry, use beige flood icing to flood the shape, then pipe an outline with cream flood icing directly into the beige icing. Using a cocktail stick, slightly swirl the 2 colours together.

3. Place the biscuit onto a baking tray and into an oven set to the lowest temperature (50°C/gas mark ¼) for 40 minutes, or until the icing has set hard.

4. To finish, pipe a line of beige line icing, following the 'bread' shape, to give the effect of a crust. Allow to fully dry.

Mug

Line: white
Flood: white / red

1. Using white line icing, pipe a mug shape on your biscuit. Pipe a thin line at the top of biscuit to create the mug's lip, then pipe 3 horizontal lines across the mug. Don't forget to pipe a handle! Leave to dry for 10 minutes at room temperature.

2. Once dry, flood the bottom section of the mug with white flood icing, then the section above with red flood icing; repeat to fill the top two sections. Flood the handle of your mug with white flood icing.

3. Place the biscuit onto a baking tray and into an oven set to the lowest temperature (50°C/gas mark ¼) for 40 minutes, or until the icing has set hard.

4. Once your biscuit has dried, you could ice the name of a friend on top, or even what you'd like your mug to contain.

Après-Ski

What could be more chic than a vintage ski get-up?
An iced biscuit version, that's what. This oh-so-cool
collection makes the most unique present for the ski
bunny in your life, or a memorable thank you for
that holiday in the mountains.

You will need:

1 batch of shaped biscuits (recipes pp.19–25)

1 batch of Royal Icing (recipe p.30), divided into line
and flood consistencies (colours detailed in individual
biscuit instructions)

Hot cocoa mug

Line: red / white
Flood: red / brown

1. Using red line icing, pipe the outline of a mug on your
   biscuit, defining the handle and creating an ellipse
   shape at the top. Leave to dry for 10 minutes at
   room temperature.

2. Once dry, flood the main part of the mug and the handle
   with red flood icing, and the ellipse with brown flood icing.

3. Place the biscuit onto a baking tray and into an oven set to
   the lowest temperature (50°C/gas mark ¼) for 40 minutes,
   or until the icing has set hard.

4. With red line icing, pipe around the outline of the mug
   to define the shape. Then, using white line icing, pipe
   small squares on top of the brown icing to look like
   marshmallows! Allow to fully dry.

Skis

Line: navy blue / white
Flood: navy blue / red

1. Using navy blue line icing, pipe two long rectangles side
   by side on your biscuits, piping the shapes into curved
   points at one end. Near the top of the skis, pipe an
   upside-down V shape on each, then repeat close to
   the bottom of the skis. Leave to dry for 10 minutes
   at room temperature.

2. Once dry, fill the middle section of your outline with navy
   flood icing. Then fill the top and bottom sections with red
   flood icing.

3. Place the biscuit onto a baking tray and into an oven
   set to the lowest temperature (50°C/gas mark ¼) for
   40 minutes, or until the icing has set hard.

4. Using white line icing, pipe 1 or 2 upside-down V shapes,
   to separate the red sections from the navy section.

5. With white line icing, pipe a small oval in the centre of
   each ski, and then two navy lines across the centre of each
   oval – this will create the foot straps! Allow to fully dry.

Bobble hat

Line: cream / red / navy blue
Flood: cream

1. Using cream-coloured line icing, pipe the outline of
   a hat on your biscuit in a semi-circle shape. Leave to dry
   for 10 minutes at room temperature.

2. Once dry, flood the hat shape with cream flood icing.

3. Place the biscuit onto a baking tray and into an oven set to
   the lowest temperature (50°C/gas mark ¼) for 40 minutes,
   or until the icing has set hard.

4. Use red line icing to pipe a thick horizontal line near
   the bottom of the hat.

5. Using cream line icing, pipe vertical lines in a back-and-
   forth motion for the rim of the hat, and a cluster of dots
   at the top of the hat for the bobble.

6. Finally, use navy line icing to pipe a thin line either side
   of the red line and add a line of navy dots across the red
   line. Allow to fully dry.

Jolly Gingers in Onesies

Our family of Jolly Gingers is ever growing, as we dream up characters for our friends and their life milestones. We have graduation gingers, doctor gingers and even an astronaut! This ginger gang are warmly onesie-clad for winter. Once you master the technique, you too can create your own motley crew of Jolly Ginger characters.

You will need:

1 batch of shaped All-Spice Biscuits (recipe p.20)

1 batch of Royal Icing (recipe p.30), line consistency, in the following colours:

dark brown / white / baby pink / hot pink / turquoise / lime green / grey

Stripy onesie

1. Add a smile and eyes to your jolly ginger, using dark-brown line icing.

2. Outline around the arms with white line icing, then use dark-brown line icing to define the hands.

3. Give your jolly ginger a white onesie using line icing. Create a stripy pattern using white, baby pink, hot pink and turquoise horizontal lines across the onesie. Add a zip and cuff details in turquoise and a white collar. Allow to fully dry.

Star onesie

1. Add a smile and eyes to your jolly ginger, using dark-brown line icing.

2. Pipe the outline of the onesie shape in grey line icing. Don't forget to ice space for the hands near the middle of the jolly ginger's tummy. Ice the hands using dark-brown line icing.

3. Using white line icing, pipe cuffs and a button-down collar.

4. Fill in the body/onesie shape with grey line icing. Leave to dry for 10 minutes at room temperature.

5. Using lime-green line icing, pipe stars all over the jolly ginger to create a fun pattern. Add a few dots for buttons.

6. Leave to fully dry at room temperature before storing or sharing with friends.

Fairy Lights Bunting

Nothing cheers up a dark winter's evening more
than a twinkly string of lights. We've sprinkled
sugar over the icing whilst wet to create this
shimmery set of lights. Once dry, simply thread
a ribbon through and they're ready to hang.

You will need:

1 batch of shaped biscuits* (Vanilla Biscuit recipe p.19)

1 batch of Royal Icing (recipe p.30), divided into line
and flood consistencies in the following colours:

*Line: orange / hot pink / green / light pink /
yellow / navy / purple / pale blue / pale green /
white / grey*

*Flood: orange / hot pink / green / light pink /
yellow / navy / purple / pale blue /
pale green / white / grey*

White granulated sugar

Ribbon

* Don't forget to cut a medium-sized hole towards the
top of the biscuits, before baking, so you can thread your
ribbon through later. You can do this with a toothpick.

1. Outline the shape of your lightbulbs on the biscuits in your
   selected colour of line icing. Outline the screw section with
   grey line icing, remembering to pipe a circle around the
   hole. Leave to dry for 10 minutes at room temperature.

2. Once dry, flood the light sections with your colour of
   flood icing and flood the screw sections with grey flood.

3. While still wet, sprinkle granulated sugar over the
   lightbulb sections to make them look sparkly and frosted.

4. Place the biscuits onto a baking tray and into an oven
   set to the lowest temperature (50°C/gas mark ¼) for
   40 minutes, or until the icing has set hard.

5. Add three horizontal lines of grey line icing to define
   the screw. Don't ice over the hole for the ribbon!
   Allow to fully dry.

6. Cut a long strip of ribbon and, using a toothpick,
   push the ribbon through the hole in one of the biscuits.
   Once the ribbon has been pushed through, tie the ribbon
   in a knot to secure, then continue in this way until all the
   biscuits have been threaded.

Hot Chocolate Toppers

The perfect baking project for those dark winter afternoons, these cute-as-a-button gingerbread houses are designed to sit neatly on top of a steaming mug of hot chocolate. We've flavoured ours with orange zest to add a festive touch, but you could use peppermint or your favourite tipple! Get creative with the houses and add personalised door numbers to give as gifts.

You will need:

½ batch of All-Spice Biscuit dough (recipe p.20)

½ batch of Royal Icing (recipe p.30), line consistency, with a small amount coloured beige

Mini gingerbread houses

1. Preheat oven to 150°C/130°C fan/gas mark 2. Line a baking tray with greaseproof paper.

2. Roll out your biscuit dough (see method on p.15), chill for 30 minutes, then cut out your panel shapes:
   2 x side walls: rectangle W5cm x H3.5cm
   2 x roof panels: rectangle W7cm x H4cm
   2 x front/back walls, with a triangular elevation and a rectangular slot cut out: W5cm x H3.5cm (triangular elevation to H6cm)

3. Carefully lift each panel onto the lined baking tray. Space each panel apart, as they may spread while cooking.

4. Bake in the hot oven for 20 minutes, then remove the biscuits from the oven, carefully transfer the sheet of greaseproof paper to a cooling rack and let the biscuits cool completely.

5. Meanwhile, prepare your white line icing.

6. Use the white and beige line icings to pipe fun designs on the walls and roof: swirls, dots, stripes, snowflakes or stars work well.

7. It's time to construct your house. Using your white line icing, pipe a line along the shorter side of each of the side panels, then attach to the front panel and back panel. Let this dry for 10 minutes at room temperature.

8. Once the side panels have dried and the structure seems sturdy, you can add the roof. Pipe a line on the apex of the roof, then add the two roof panels, holding them in place for around 3–4 minutes until they dry. Finally, pipe along the ridge of the roof, for extra strength.

Orange hot chocolate

Makes enough for 2 large mugs

1 pint milk

50g dark orange chocolate, chopped

zest of ½ orange

1. In a heavy-based saucepan set over a low heat, gently heat the milk.

2. Once the milk has come to a low boil, stir in the chocolate and zest with a balloon whisk, stirring until fully incorporated with no lumps. If you want to add an orange liqueur you can add it now.

3. Pour equal amounts of your hot chocolate into two mugs and finish with a gingerbread-house topper of course!

Themes

Fashionista

Lights, camera, action! The fashion world is an endless source of inspiration for us and we have honed our icing skills creating designs for some of the world's most famous fashion brands. Ice your very own collection of catwalk creations for the fashionista in your life, a unique gift that will never go out of style.

You will need:

1 batch of shaped biscuits (recipes pp.19–25)

1 batch of Royal Icing (recipe p.30), divided into line and flood consistencies (colours detailed in individual biscuit instructions)

Edible bronze shimmer paint

Trench coat

Line: cream / black
Flood: cream / beige

1. Use cream line icing to pipe the outline of the trench coat on the biscuit, with a tear-drop shape at the top for the neck. Leave to dry for 10 minutes at room temperature.

2. Once dry, flood the main section of the biscuit with cream flood icing, and flood the neck of the biscuit with beige flood icing.

3. Place the biscuit onto a baking tray and into an oven set to the lowest temperature (50°C/gas mark ¼) for 40 minutes, or until the icing has set hard.

4. Use cream line icing to pipe the jacket details and black line icing to pipe the buttons and buckles. Allow to dry.

Lipstick

Line: beige / red or pink / white
Flood: beige

1. Use beige line icing to pipe the shape of the lipstick tube on the biscuit. Leave to dry for 10 minutes at room temperature.

2. Once dry, flood the lipstick tube with beige flood icing.

3. Place the biscuit onto a baking tray and into an oven set to the lowest temperature (50°C/gas mark ¼) for 40 minutes, or until the icing has set hard.

4. Using beige line icing, pipe the ridges and detail on the lipstick tube. Leave to dry for 10 minutes.

5. Using a small paint brush, brush the edible bronze paint over the tube of the lipstick and allow to dry.

6. Use pink or red line icing to pipe the tip of the lipstick, filling in with a back-and-forth motion. Dry for 10 minutes.

7. Finish with little lines of white line icing, to add the effect of a shine to the tube and lipstick. Allow to fully dry.

Jumper

Line: baby pink / white / green
Flood: baby pink / white

1. Use baby pink line icing to pipe the shape of a jumper on the biscuit. Pipe 2 lines across the chest, to create a horizontal stripe, and a line across the bottom of the sleeves and jumper. Leave to dry for 10 minutes at room temperature.

2. Once dry, flood the sleeves and the main part of the jumper with baby pink flood icing. Flood the bottom of the sleeves, jumper and the stripe with white flood.

3. Place the biscuit onto a baking tray and into an oven set to the lowest temperature (50°C/gas mark ¼) for 40 minutes, or until the icing has set hard.

4. Add some definition to the sleeves, neck and arms of the jumper with baby pink line icing. Outline the horizontal stripe with white line icing.

5. Pipe a heart with green line icing in the middle of the stripe.

6. Using a small paint brush, lightly brush the edible bronze paint on to the bottom of the sleeves and the jumper. Allow to fully dry.

Movie Night

Ice our movie-inspired biscuits for your favourite film geek and you'll win the Oscar for Best Gift Giver! The cute popcorn biscuits are certain to get a five-star review from everyone you know.

You will need:

1 batch of shaped biscuits (recipes pp.19–25)

1 batch of Royal Icing (recipe p.30), divided into line and flood consistencies (colours detailed in individual biscuit instructions)

Popcorn and box

Line: red / cream
Flood: red / white

1. Using red line icing, pipe the outline of your box, with a scalloped top and 4 vertical lines down the biscuit. Leave to dry for 10 minutes at room temperature.

2. Once dry, using red flood icing, flood the centre section and outer sections. Then flood the remaining 2 sections with white flood icing.

3. Place the biscuit onto a baking tray and into an oven set to the lowest temperature (50°C/gas mark ¼) for 40 minutes, or until the icing has set hard.

4. Use cream line icing to pipe little swirls all over the top of the biscuit to look like fluffy popcorn. Allow to fully dry.

3-D glasses

Line: black / white
Flood: black / blue / red

1. Using black line icing, pipe the outline of frames on the biscuit. Leave to dry for 10 minutes at room temperature.

2. Once dry, flood the frames with black flood icing, then flood one lens with blue flood and the other with red flood.

3. Place the biscuit onto a baking tray and into an oven set to the lowest temperature (50°C/gas mark ¼) for 40 minutes, or until the icing has set hard.

4. Use white line icing to pipe a small curved line and dot in each lens for a shine effect. Allow to fully dry.

Individual popcorn

Line: cream
Flood: cream / beige

1. Using cream line icing, pipe the outline of your popcorn onto a circular biscuit. Leave to dry for 10 minutes at room temperature.

2. Once dry, flood the popcorn with cream flood icing. While the icing is still wet, pipe a few random lines of beige flood icing directly into the cream flood.

3. Place the biscuit onto a baking tray and into an oven set to the lowest temperature (50°C/gas mark ¼) for 40 minutes, or until the icing has set hard.

4. Use cream line icing to add detail and pipe down the edge of each beige line. Allow to fully dry.

Hot dog

Line: brown / cream / red / yellow
Flood: brown / cream

1. Using brown line icing, pipe the outline of a sausage horizontally across the centre of your biscuit. Then, either side of the sausage, pipe the outline of a hot-dog bun with cream line icing. Leave to dry for 10 minutes at room temperature.

2. Once dry, flood the sausage with brown flood icing, then flood the hot-dog bun with cream line icing.

3. Place the biscuit onto a baking tray and into an oven set to the lowest temperature (50°C/gas mark ¼) for 40 minutes, or until the icing has set hard.

4. Use brown line icing to outline the sausage. Then, across the centre of the sausage, pipe a wiggly line of red line icing (ketchup) and a wiggly line of yellow line icing (mustard). Allow to fully dry.

Sushi

Roll up, roll up! This witty collection is a homage to our favourite food and will look super *kawaii* served at your dinner party. Sushi for even the fussiest of folk – chopsticks optional!

You will need:

1 batch of shaped biscuits (recipes pp.19–25)

1 batch of Royal Icing (recipe p.30), divided into line and flood consistencies (colours detailed in individual biscuit instructions)

Soy sauce 'fish' *(top)*

Line: green / brown / white
Flood: green / brown

1. Using green line icing, pipe a tiny rectangle at the front of your biscuit (for the cap) and pipe an oval shape beside it in brown line icing. Leave to dry for 10 minutes at room temperature.

2. Once dry, flood the cap with green and the oval with brown flood icing.

3. Place the biscuit onto a baking tray and into an oven set to the lowest temperature (50°C/gas mark ¼) for 40 minutes, or until the icing has set hard.

4. Pipe an eye, mouth and gills with brown line icing, then use white line icing to pipe a tail and fins to finish the biscuit. Allow to fully dry.

Nigiri *(middle)*

Line: white / orange
Flood: orange / white

1. Using white line icing, pipe the outline of the rice section on the biscuit. Then, using orange line icing, pipe the outline of the prawn. Leave to dry for 10 minutes at room temperature.

2. Once dry, flood the prawn section in orange flood icing and the rice section in white flood.

3. Place the biscuit onto a baking tray and into an oven set to the lowest temperature (50°C/gas mark ¼) for 40 minutes, or until the icing has set hard.

4. Use orange and white line icing to add definition and shape to the prawn.

5. Pipe little white lines across the white section of your biscuit to give the effect of rice. Allow to fully dry.

Maki roll *(second from bottom)*

Line: black / white / green / orange
Flood: white / black

1. Using black line icing, pipe a tube shape on the biscuit (with an oval shape at the top). Leave to dry for 10 minutes at room temperature.

2. Once dry, flood the top oval section with white flood icing and the bottom section with black flood icing.

3. Place the biscuit onto a baking tray and into an oven set to the lowest temperature (50°C/gas mark ¼) for 40 minutes, or until the icing has set hard.

4. Using black line icing, pipe four thin curved lines on the right of the biscuit, to give the illusion of a curved side.

5. Using a mixture of green, white and orange line icings, pipe the rice and 'filling' of the sushi on top of the white iced section. Allow to fully dry.

Afternoon Tea

Quintessentially British, our intricate porcelain tea set is finished with delicate dots of icing and painted gold. Present on a vintage saucer and serve with a pot of Earl Grey for the ultimate afternoon tea.

You will need:

1 batch of shaped biscuits (recipes pp.19–25)

1 batch of Royal Icing (recipe p.30), divided into line and flood consistencies in the following colours:

Line: cream / turquoise / white / grey blue

Flood: cream / turquoise / white / grey blue

Edible gold shimmer paint

Tea cups

1. Pipe the outline of tea cups on the biscuits with a coloured line icing of your choice. Pipe the base of the tea cup and body and then a curved dip at the top. At this stage, you can pipe a horizontal line across the centre of your teacup, if you wish, to have 2 flood colours. Leave to dry for 10 minutes at room temperature.

2. Once dry, flood the body of the tea cup with your chosen colour/s.

3. Place the biscuits onto a baking tray and into an oven set to the lowest temperature (50°C/gas mark ¼) for 40 minutes, or until the icing has set hard.

4. Take a line icing and pipe the handle of the teacup and a line across the top edge of your biscuit to create the lip of the teacup.

5. At this stage, you can add any extra piped details you wish, such as a line across the centre of the cup, to add definition, if you chose to use 2 flood colours, or dots and swirls. Let the icing dry for 10 minutes.

6. Now for the fun bit! Dip a clean paintbrush into the edible gold paint and carefully paint over the line icing details. For further decoration, you can also paint directly onto the flood icing – floral designs, decorative swirls, dots or stripes. Allow to fully dry.

Tea pots

1. Pipe the outline of your teapots on the biscuits with a coloured line icing of your choice. Pipe the base of the teapot and the round body, being sure to outline the spout and lid. At this stage, you can pipe a scalloped line across the centre of the teapot if you wish to have 2 flood colours. Leave to dry for 10 minutes at room temperature.

2. Once dry, flood the body of the teapot with your chosen colour/s.

3. Place the biscuits onto a baking tray and into an oven set to the lowest temperature (50°C/gas mark ¼) for 40 minutes, or until the icing has set hard.

4. Take a line icing and pipe the handle of your teapot and a line across the top to create the lid of the teapot.

5. At this stage, add any line detail that you would like to – pipe dots, lines, waved patterns, be as creative as you like! You may also want to pipe along the dividing line if you chose to use 2 flood colours. Let the icing dry for 10 minutes.

6. Dip a clean paintbrush into the edible gold paint and carefully paint over the line icing details. Adding different design elements to each section of the biscuit will help to separate the sections of the teapot – try painting small dots on the lid, and contrasting swirls or flowers onto the body of the teapot. Allow to fully dry.

Patisserie

Wobbling jellies, mini macarons and a towering croquembouche, this collection is inspired by fancy French patisserie. There are some tricky techniques and a lot of line work, but if you can master it they make *le meilleur cadeau anniversaire. Ooh la la!*

You will need:

1 batch of shaped biscuits (recipes pp.19–25)

1 batch of Royal Icing (recipe p.30), divided into line and flood consistencies (colours detailed in individual biscuit instructions)

Croquembouche

Line: white / beige / lime green / dark pink / light pink
Flood: white / beige

1. Use white line icing to pipe the long, curved oval outline of the tray at the bottom of your biscuit.

2. Above this, pipe 6 rows of small circles in beige line icing. Start with 6 in a row, then pipe 5 in the next row, reducing to 1 on the top. Leave to dry for 10 minutes.

3. When dry, flood the tray outline with white flood icing and the circles with beige flood icing – don't over-fill!

4. Place the biscuit onto a baking tray and into an oven set to the lowest temperature (50°C/gas mark ¼) for 40 minutes, or until the icing has set hard.

5. Use white line icing to pipe a scalloped pattern across the tray and a row of white dots underneath each scallop.

6. Finally, alternate between white, lime green, dark and light pink line icing to pipe small clusters of dots in-between the layers of beige circles. Allow to fully dry.

Pink jelly

Line: white / dark pink / light pink / lime green
Flood: white / dark pink / light pink

1. Use white line icing to pipe the long, curved oval outline of the tray at the bottom of your biscuit.

2. Above the tray, pipe a slightly shorter oval with dark pink line icing.

3. On top of this, alternate between light and dark pink line icing to pipe 5 long vertical oval segments. Leave to dry for 10 minutes.

4. When dry, flood the tray outline with white flood icing, the segment above with dark pink flood icing and the vertical segments with the same colour flood as the respective outer line.

5. Place the biscuit onto a baking tray and into an oven set to the lowest temperature (50°C/gas mark ¼) for 40 minutes, or until the icing has set hard.

6. Use white line icing to pipe a zig-zag pattern across the tray. Outline the jelly segments with the matching colour of line icing.

7. Finally, using light pink line icing, pipe a cluster of dots on the top of the jelly and then a short green line, to represent a cluster of berries. Allow to fully dry.

Cupcake stand

Line: white / hot pink / beige / lime green / light pink / warm pink
Flood: white

1. Using white line icing, pipe the outline of the base and stand. Leave to dry for 10 minutes.

2. When dry, flood the base and stand with white flood icing.

3. Place the biscuit onto a baking tray and into an oven set to the lowest temperature (50°C/gas mark ¼) for 40 minutes, or until the icing has set hard.

4. Use white line icing to pipe a scallop pattern across the base and at the bottom of the stand. In the centre of the stand pipe a small heart.

5. Use hot pink, beige and lime green line icing to pipe three cupcake cases on top of the base.

6. Use beige, light pink and warm pink line icing to pipe the domes of the cupcakes. Finish off the cupcakes with a dot of hot pink icing on the top.

7. Finally, using white line icing, pipe the outline of the tall dome and add a small dot on the top for a handle. Allow to fully dry.

Cycling

This collection is inspired by our cycling-obsessed pals and their love for the open road. Ice your very own peloton of cyclists for your favourite race enthusiast – you could even ice their initials onto the yellow-jersey rider for extra points.

You will need:

1 batch of shaped biscuits (recipes pp.19–25)

1 batch of Royal Icing (recipe p.30), divided into line and flood consistencies, in the following colours:

Line: yellow / beige or brown / black / blue / grey

Flood: yellow / beige or brown

1. Using yellow line icing, outline the shape of an almond at the top of the biscuit – this will be the cyclist's helmet.

2. Then pipe a small circle underneath with beige or brown line icing – this will be the cyclist's head.

3. With yellow line icing, pipe a curved line along the outer edge for the cyclist's back, continue this line down and pipe the shape of a leg, moving back up, mirroring the outer curve, to create the torso. Then pipe the arm coming down to the handlebars.

4. Pipe a line to define the cyclist's waist, and then another further down to define the shorts and a line to define the jersey arm. Leave to dry for 10 minutes.

5. Once dry, flood the helmet, jersey and shorts with yellow flood icing.

6. Using beige or brown flood icing, flood the head, arm and leg sections.

7. Place the biscuits onto a baking tray and into an oven set to the lowest temperature (50°C/gas mark ¼) for 40 minutes, or until the icing has set hard.

8. Pipe the jersey details with blue line icing. Then pipe a yellow line across the top of the shorts for definition.

9. Using black line icing, pipe a set of horizontal stripes across the helmet, then pipe a set of handles under the cyclist's hands. Then pipe 2 large circles at the bottom of the biscuit for the bike's tyres.

10. Pipe a circle of yellow line icing within the inner edge of each of the black circles, then continue to pipe the frame and seat of the bike.

11. Use black line icing to pipe the cyclist's shoe and add detail to the bike seat.

12. Finally, use grey line icing to pipe spokes coming from the centre of each wheel. Allow to fully dry.

TOP TIP – *You can reverse the colour of the icing on your biscuits. Try adding extra detail to your jerseys with piped dots and stripes in reds and greens or white.*

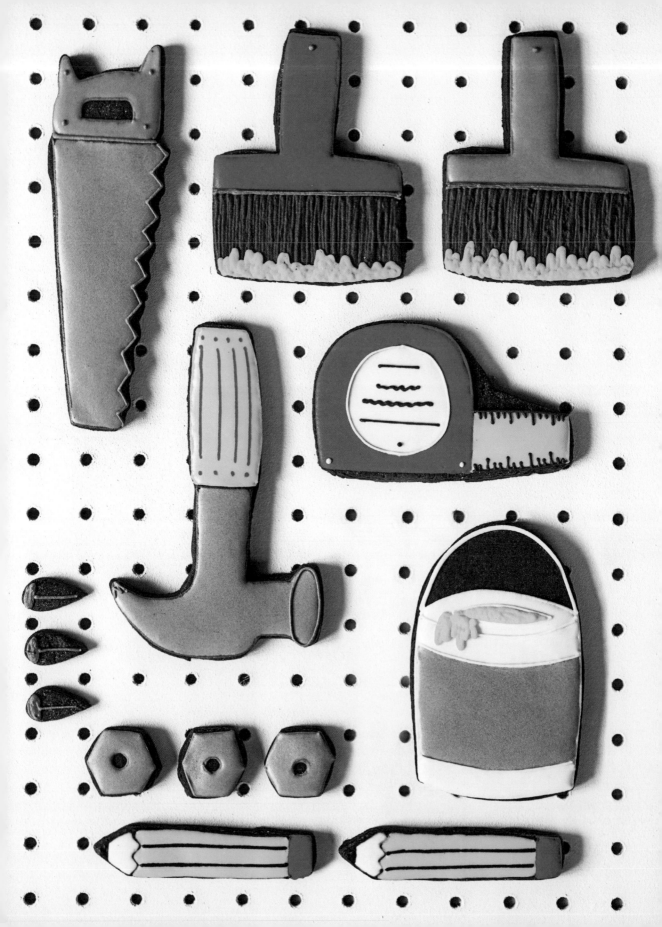

Tool Kit

For the DIY hero in your life, whether that be dad, sister, husband or neighbour, this box of tools is the sweetest way to say thank you for giving up their Saturday afternoon. Master the art of writing with a piping bag, p.38, and personalise the paint pot with a special message.

You will need:

1 batch of shaped biscuits (recipes pp.19–25)

1 batch of Royal Icing (recipe p.30), divided into line and flood consistencies (colours detailed in individual biscuit instructions)

Edible silver paint

Paint brush

Line: red or blue / brown / yellow / grey
Flood: red or blue

1. Pipe the outline of the paint-brush handle in red or blue line icing. Leave to dry for 10 minutes at room temperature.

2. Once dry, flood the handle with red or blue flood icing.

3. Place the biscuit onto a baking tray and into an oven set to the lowest temperature (50°C/gas mark ¼) for 40 minutes, or until the icing has set hard.

4. Using brown line icing, pipe lots of lines to look like the bristles of the brush. Leave to dry for 10 minutes.

5. Use yellow line icing to pipe drips on top of the bristles to look like yellow paint.

6. Pipe a thick line of grey line icing where the brush and bristles meet and a small a dot at the top of the handle. Leave to dry for 10 minutes.

7. Once dry, take a clean brush, dip it in edible silver paint and carefully paint over the grey line and dot for a metallic finish. Allow to fully dry.

Hammer

Line: grey / yellow / red
Flood: grey / yellow

1. Using grey line icing, pipe the head of the hammer on the biscuit. Outline the handle with yellow line icing. Leave to dry for 10 minutes at room temperature.

2. Once dry, flood the hammer head with grey flood icing and the handle with yellow flood.

3. Place the biscuit onto a baking tray and into an oven set to the lowest temperature (50°C/gas mark ¼) for 40 minutes, or until the icing has set hard.

4. Using red line icing, pipe several lines on the handle of the hammer, with a dot at either end.

5. Use grey line icing to add detail to the head of the hammer. Allow to fully dry.

Saw

Line: blue / grey
Flood: blue / grey

1. Pipe the outline of a saw handle on the biscuit with blue line icing and a saw blade with grey line icing. Leave to dry for 10 minutes at room temperature.

2. Once dry, flood the handle with blue flood icing and the blade with grey flood.

3. Place the biscuit onto a baking tray and into an oven set to the lowest temperature (50°C/gas mark ¼) for 40 minutes, or until the icing has set hard.

4. Use grey line icing to outline the blade and pipe 4 dots on the corners of the saw handle. Allow to fully dry.

Camping

There's nothing quite like hiking in the great outdoors, picking the best camping spot and settling in for an evening under the stars. This collection is our homage to many a summer night spent under canvas, the perfect gift for any adventure-loving friend.

You will need:

1 batch of shaped biscuits (recipes pp.19–25)

Wooden skewers (for Marshmallow Stick, see step 1)

1 batch of Royal Icing (recipe p.30), divided into line and flood consistencies (colours detailed in individual biscuit instructions)

Tent

Line: green / navy blue / white / beige
Flood: green / navy blue / white

1. Using green line icing, pipe the outline of a V shape at the bottom of the biscuit. Use navy blue to continue the side lines up to the point of a triangle at the top. Don't forget to add a square on the left-hand side for the window. Leave to dry for 10 minutes at room temperature.

2. Once dry, flood the lower V shape with green flood icing and the top section with navy flood. Fill in the window shape with white flood.

3. Place the biscuit onto a baking tray and into an oven set to the lowest temperature (50°C/gas mark ¼) for 40 minutes, or until the icing has set hard.

4. Pipe 4 lines of beige line icing at the top of the tent for poles.

5. Use navy line icing to frame the window and add a cross in the middle. Add a triangle shape to define the tent panels.

6. Finally, use white line icing to add zig-zags across the bottom section for a funky pattern. Allow to fully dry.

Marshmallow stick

Line: white
Flood: white / beige

1. Make your dough and cut into rectangle shapes. Before placing in the oven for baking, carefully thread wooden skewers through the length of the rectangle (see pp.15–16 for baking instructions).

2. Once biscuits are baked and cooled, use white line icing to pipe the outline of 3 marshmallow shapes on the biscuits. Leave to dry at room temperature for 10 minutes.

3. Once dry, flood the shapes with white flood icing and add 3 splodges of beige flood icing in each marshmallow shape.

4. Use a cocktail stick to swirl the colours together.

5. Place the biscuits onto a baking tray and into an oven set to the lowest temperature (50°C/gas mark ¼) for 40 minutes, or until the icing has set hard.

6. Define the edges of each marshmallow with white line icing. Allow to fully dry.

Campfire

Line: orange / brown
Flood: orange / yellow / brown

1. Pipe a fire shape in orange line icing and 6 logs in brown line icing on the biscuit. Leave to dry at room temperature for 10 minutes.

2. Once dry, use a mixture of orange and yellow flood icings to fill in the fire section. Swirl together with a cocktail stick.

3. Flood the log shapes with brown flood icing.

4. Place the biscuit onto a baking tray and into an oven set to the lowest temperature (50°C/gas mark ¼) for 40 minutes, or until the icing has set hard.

5. Outline the edge of the logs and add small line details in brown line icing to create texture. Allow to fully dry.

Best of British

London is our stomping ground and an endless source of inspiration for our biscuits. We've celebrated royal weddings and the jubilee with extra special designs and collectable tins. You'll be crowned 'best neighbour' at any street party with this collection up your sleeve.

You will need:

1 batch of shaped biscuits (recipes pp.19–25)

1 batch of Royal Icing (recipe p.30), divided into line and flood consistencies (colours detailed in individual biscuit instructions)

Granulated sugar (for Crown biscuits)

Bunting

Line: light blue / red / white
Flood: light blue

1. Use light blue line icing to pipe the outline of your biscuits. Leave to dry for 10 minutes at room temperature.

2. Once dry, flood the biscuits with light blue flood icing.

3. Place the biscuits onto a baking tray and into an oven set to the lowest temperature (50°C/gas mark ¼) for 40 minutes, or until the icing has set hard.

4. Use red line icing to pipe a red cross, and then outline with white line icing either side. Use white line icing to add a diagonal line in each blue section of your bunting. Allow to fully dry.

Crown

Line: white

1. Use white line icing to pipe the crown shape onto your biscuit. Don't forget to add details, such as dots around the top edge, and a cross.

2. While the icing is wet, sprinkle over some sugar and leave to dry at room temperature for 10 minutes. Carefully tap off any excess sugar when dry.

Queen's guard

Line: black / red / cream / white / beige
Flood: cream / black / red

1. Pipe the guard's bearskin onto the biscuit with black line icing and outline his trousers. Pipe a jacket shape with red line icing and the outline of the head in cream line icing. Leave to dry for 10 minutes at room temperature.

2. Once dry, flood the head shape with cream flood icing, the trousers and bearskin with black flood and the jacket with red flood.

3. Place the biscuit onto a baking tray and into an oven set to the lowest temperature (50°C/gas mark ¼) for 40 minutes, or until the icing has set hard.

4. Use red line icing to define the jacket sleeves and waist and white line icing to ice the buttons and central line.

5. Use beige line icing to pipe a chin strap, hands and epaulettes. Add dots of black for the eyes. Allow to dry.

Rainbows and Unicorns

Always be yourself, unless you can be a unicorn. Then always be a unicorn! Something of an Instagram star, our unicorns create happiness wherever they go. Spread your own bit of magic with this great starter project. There's very little line icing to do, but it creates maximum impact.

You will need:

1 batch of shaped biscuits (recipes pp.19–25)

1 batch of Royal Icing (recipe p.30), divided into line and flood consistencies (colours detailed in individual biscuit instructions)

Unicorn

Line: white / black / hot pink / yellow / lime green / blue
Flood: white

1. Use white line icing to pipe the outline of the body and horn of your unicorn on the biscuit. Leave to dry for 10 minutes at room temperature.

2. Once dry, flood the shape with white flood icing – don't over-fill!

3. Place the biscuit onto a baking tray and into an oven set to the lowest temperature (50°C/gas mark ¼) for 40 minutes, or until the icing has set hard.

4. Use black line icing to give the unicorn a dot for a nose and a small curve for an eye.

5. Use hot pink line icing to give the unicorn hooves and a fringe.

6. Use white line icing to pipe a zig-zag line on the horn, for definition.

7. Finally, use a mixture of bright line colours to pipe your unicorn's magical mane and tail. Allow to fully dry.

Rainbow

Line: blue / lime green / yellow / hot pink

1. Take your blue line icing and carefully ice 3 curved lines side-by-side along the bottom edge of your biscuit, to create the first layer of your rainbow.

2. Repeat this step with green, then yellow line icing, and finish off with 3 lines of hot pink along the top edge.

3. Leave your biscuits to dry at room temperature for 15 minutes, until the icing has completely set.

Star

Line: bright colours of choice
Flood: bright colours of choice

1. Pipe the outline of your star biscuits using a brightly coloured line icing of your choice. Leave to dry for 10 minutes at room temperature.

2. Once dry, flood your stars with brightly coloured flood icings of your choice.

3. Place the biscuits onto a baking tray and into an oven set to the lowest temperature (50°C/gas mark ¼) for 40 minutes, or until the icing has set hard.

Safari

This rather classy collection of wild animals will be a memorable gift for the David Attenborough in your life. A grrr-reat welcome-home gift from their latest safari adventure!

You will need:

1 batch of shaped biscuits (recipes pp.19–25)

1 batch of Royal Icing (recipe p.30), divided into line and flood consistencies (colours detailed in individual biscuit instructions)

Elephant

Line: grey / black / white
Flood: grey

1. Pipe the outline of the elephant on your biscuit with grey line icing. Leave to dry for 10 minutes at room temperature.

2. Once dry, flood the shape with grey flood icing.

3. Place the biscuit onto a baking tray and into an oven set to the lowest temperature (50°C/gas mark ¼) for 40 minutes, or until the icing has set hard.

4. Use grey line icing to outline the elephant again, then pipe the ear, the tail and a small curved line for an eyelid.

5. Pipe a large black dot directly under the eyelid and add a small dot of white on top.

6. Finally, use white to pipe a tusk and 3 dots at the bottom of each leg for the elephant's toes. Allow to fully dry.

Giraffe

Line: beige / brown / black / white
Flood: beige / brown

1. Pipe the outline of the giraffe's head on the biscuit with beige line icing, outlining an ear and both 'horns'. Leave to dry for 10 minutes at room temperature.

2. Once dry, flood the shape with beige flood icing and, while the icing is still wet, pipe various-sized splodges of brown flood icing directly into the beige icing.

3. Use a cocktail stick to very slightly drag out the edges of the brown splodges to distort the shapes.

4. Place the biscuit onto a baking tray and into an oven set to the lowest temperature (50°C/gas mark ¼) for 40 minutes, or until the icing has set hard.

5. Use brown line icing to pipe the mouth, jaw, upper eyelid and a cluster of tiny dots at the top of each 'horn'.

6. Use black line icing to pipe a nostril and a large dot under the eyelid. Then pipe a small curve of white line icing on the side of the black to define the eye.

7. Finally, use beige line icing to pipe definition for the ear, chin and forehead. Allow to fully dry.

Lion

Line: beige / brown / black / white
Flood: beige

1. Using beige line icing, pipe the outline of the lion's body, feet and head onto the biscuit. Leave to dry for 10 minutes at room temperature.

2. Once dry, flood the shape with beige flood icing.

3. Place the biscuit onto a baking tray and into an oven set to the lowest temperature (50°C/gas mark ¼) for 40 minutes, or until the icing has set hard.

4. Use beige line icing to define the legs, ear, mouth and tail, and to pipe a cluster of dots on the face for whiskers.

5. Use brown line icing to pipe the tip of the tail.

6. To create the lion's mane, alternate between brown and beige line icing, piping in a back-and-forth motion.

7. Use black line icing to pipe a large dot for an eye. Then pipe a small curved line of white along the top edge of the black.

8. Finally, use white line icing to pipe a dot for a nose and 3 dots at the bottom of each leg for the claws. Allow to fully dry.

New Year's Cocktails

Whatever the occasion, these cocktail biscuits will let your party guests enjoy all of the fun, without the hangover. What could be more special than icing your friends' and family's favourite tipples, just for them? That's a whiskey sour for Grandad and a pornstar martini for Gran, then.

You will need:

1 batch of shaped biscuits (recipes pp.19–25)

1 batch of Royal Icing (recipe p.30), divided into line and flood consistencies (colours detailed in individual biscuit instructions)

Martini with olive

Line: white / light blue / red / olive green / beige
Flood: light blue / white

1. Using white line icing, pipe the base of your glass and then 2 vertical lines up the biscuit to create a thick stem. Outline the body of the glass with a 'V' shape.

2. Pipe a curved line of light blue icing parallel to the rim of the glass. Leave to dry for 10 minutes.

3. Flood the main area of the glass with light blue flood icing. Then, flood the stem and base with white flood icing.

4. Place the biscuit onto a baking tray and into an oven set to the lowest temperature (50°C/gas mark ¼) for 40 minutes, or until the icing has set hard.

5. Use white line icing to outline the body of the glass, the stem and the base. Pipe a small line and dot to one side of the glass to look like a reflection.

6. Use white line icing to pipe a large ellipse shape at the top to look like the rim of the glass.

7. Outline the top of the 'drink' with a light blue ellipse shape.

8. Pipe a small dot of red line icing close to the bottom of the drink, and then pipe a circle of olive green line icing around the red dot. Using beige line icing, pipe a line at either end of the olive for the cocktail stick. Allow to fully dry.

Negroni

Line: white / yellow / orange / beige
Flood: orange / yellow / white

1. Use white line icing to outline the base section and vertical edges of the glass on the biscuit, and then outline some ice cube shapes. Use yellow line icing to pipe the shape of a lemon slice in the middle and then use orange line icing to pipe a horizontal, slightly curved, line either side of the lemon, to create the surface of the drink. Leave to dry for 10 minutes at room temperature.

2. Once dry, flood the drink section with orange flood icing, the lemon section with yellow flood icing and the ice cubes and base with white flood.

3. Place the biscuit onto a baking tray and into an oven set to the lowest temperature (50°C/gas mark ¼) for 40 minutes, or until the icing has set hard.

4. Use white line icing to outline the sides and the rim of the glass and to redefine the ice cubes.

5. Outline the lemon and its sections with yellow line icing and pipe 2 curved lines of orange to define the surface of the drink.

6. Finally, use beige line icing to pipe a cocktail stick leaning into the glass. Allow to fully dry.

Easter Tree Collection

Every Easter, we look forward to decorating our Easter tree with gambolling lambs, hopping bunnies and cute-as-a-button chicks. Inviting each of your guests to take one home will soon become a tradition!

TOP TIP – *Long, sturdy twigs from the garden are perfect for your Easter tree – either natural or painted white. A couple of branches of pussy willow are equally as lovely.*

You will need:

1 batch of shaped biscuits* (recipes pp.19–25)

1 batch of Royal Icing (recipe p.30), divided into line and flood consistencies (colours detailed in individual biscuit instructions)

Ribbon

* Don't forget to cut a medium-sized hole towards the top of the biscuits, before baking, so you can thread your ribbons through later. Use the end of a straw to cut out the perfect-sized hole from your uncooked dough!

Lamb

Line: white / pastel green / baby pink / black

1. Using white line icing, outline the shape of a lamb on the biscuit and pipe around the cut-out hole. Leave to dry for 10 minutes at room temperature.

2. Once dry, use white line icing to pipe horizontal lines across the biscuit, with a back-and-forth motion, until the shape is full. Allow to dry for a few minutes.

3. Use pastel green line icing to pipe a line across the lamb's neck and pink line icing to give the lamb a nose. Finally, add 2 dots of black line icing for eyes. Allow to fully dry.

Chick

Line: yellow / pastel green / baby pink / black
Flood: yellow

1. Using yellow line icing, outline the shape of a chick on the biscuit and pipe around the cut-out hole. Leave to dry for 10 minutes at room temperature.

2. Once dry, flood the shape with yellow flood icing.

3. Place the biscuit onto a baking tray and into an oven set to the lowest temperature (50°C/gas mark ¼) for 40 minutes, or until the icing has set hard.

4. Use yellow line icing to pipe the chick's feet, pastel green for a bow around the chick's neck and pink for a beak. Finally, add a dot of black for an eye. Allow to fully dry.

Bunny

Line: light brown / white / yellow / baby pink / black
Flood: light brown

1. Using light brown line icing, pipe the outline of a bunny on your biscuit and pipe around the cut-out hole. Leave to dry for 10 minutes at room temperature.

2. Once dry, flood the shape with light brown flood icing.

3. Place the biscuit onto a baking tray and into an oven set to the lowest temperature (50°C/gas mark ¼) for 40 minutes, or until the icing has set hard.

4. Use white line icing to pipe the bunny's fluffy tail, yellow to pipe a bow around the bunny's neck and pink for a nose. Finally, add a dot of black for an eye. Allow to fully dry.

Fabergé Easter Eggs

Too pretty to hide in the garden, these special Fabergé-inspired biscuits make a very grown-up Easter present. The intricate line work takes some practice, so we always ice onto parchment paper first, to steady our hands. If in doubt … add more gold balls!

You will need:

1 batch of egg-shaped biscuits (recipes pp.19–25)

1 batch of Royal Icing (recipe p.30), divided into line and flood consistencies (colours detailed in individual biscuit instructions)

Granulated sugar

Edible gold ball decorations

Blue scalloped egg

Line: blue / white / beige
Flood: blue

1. Using blue line icing, pipe around the edge of the biscuit in an egg-shape. Leave to dry for 10 minutes at room temperature.

2. Once dry, flood the shape with blue flood icing.

3. Place the biscuit onto a baking tray and into an oven set to the lowest temperature (50°C/gas mark ¼) for 40 minutes, or until the icing has set hard.

4. Using white line icing, pipe a scalloped pattern across your biscuit in rows.

5. While the icing is still wet, sprinkle some sugar directly onto the icing. Gently tap off any excess.

6. In the centre of each scallop shape, use beige line icing to pipe 3 small lines in a fan shape. Allow to fully dry.

Pink latticed egg

Line: hot pink / white / beige
Flood: hot pink

1. Using hot pink line icing, pipe around the edge of the biscuit in an egg-shape. Leave to dry for 10 minutes at room temperature.

2. Once dry, flood the shape with hot pink flood icing.

3. Place the biscuit onto a baking tray and into an oven set to the lowest temperature (50°C/gas mark ¼) for 40 minutes, or until the icing has set hard.

4. Using white line icing, pipe 2 horizontal lines across the biscuit – one near the top and one near the bottom. Between the lines, pipe a set of diagonal lines one way across the biscuit, then repeat in the other direction to create a lattice effect.

5. While the icing is still wet, sprinkle some sugar directly onto the icing. Gently tap off any excess.

6. Where the diagonal lines in the lattice meet, place a gold ball decoration at the centre. If they are not sticking to the sugared line icing, pipe an extra dot of line icing onto the intersection before applying the balls.

7. Use beige line icing to pipe a fan shape at the very top and bottom of the biscuit. Allow to fully dry.

Easter Egg Nest Cake

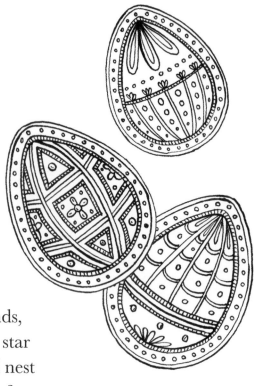

Easter is a time for hosting family and friends, and this show-stopper of a cake will be the star of your Easter Sunday feast. The shredded nest can be made with little helpers, because it's fun, messy and doesn't require an oven.

You will need:

3 x 20-cm/8-inch Super Chocolatey Cake layers (recipe p.26)

2 batches of Chocolate Buttercream (recipe p.35)

25-cm/10-inch cake board

100g dark chocolate

100g shredded-wheat-type cereal

Iced Fabergé Easter Egg biscuits (recipe p.115)

1. Bake your cakes according to the recipe. Once the cake layers are completely cool, you can begin to stack them up. Using a sharp knife, carefully level the top of each layer – they will need to sit flat.

2. Smear a little buttercream onto the cake board and place the first cake layer on top, to secure it to the board.

3. Using a palette knife, spread the buttercream evenly over the top of the first layer, then place another cake layer on top. Repeat.

4. Take a generous amount of buttercream and smooth it around the edge of the cake. Scrape off the excess until the cake is evenly covered in buttercream.

5. Drag a fork through the surface of the buttercream to create texture – you want to create the effect of tree bark.

6. In a heatproof bowl set over a saucepan of gently simmering water, melt the dark chocolate (ensure the bottom of the bowl does not touch the water). When melted, mix in the shredded-wheat cereal and leave to one side to cool slightly.

7. When the chocolate cereal mixture is cool enough to handle, carefully mould a ring of it around the top of the cake to form a 'nest'.

8. Finish off by placing some of your iced Fabergé Easter Egg biscuits inside the nest.

Diwali

Diwali is the festival of light, celebrated with the lighting of thousands of lanterns, which glimmer into the new-moon night. Traditionally, sweets are given to loved ones and this colourful collection is the perfect way to celebrate.

You will need:

1 batch of shaped biscuits (recipes pp.19–25)

1 batch of Royal Icing (recipe p.30), divided into line and flood consistencies (colours detailed in individual biscuit instructions)

Diya oil candle

Line: yellow / orange / dark pink / black
Flood: yellow / orange

1. Use yellow line icing to pipe a large teardrop shape in the middle of the biscuit. Then use orange line icing to pipe a boat-like shape underneath – this should fill about half of the biscuit. Leave to dry for 10 minutes at room temperature.

2. Once dry, flood the teardrop with yellow flood icing and the 'boat' with orange flood icing.

3. Place the biscuit onto a baking tray and into an oven set to the lowest temperature (50°C/gas mark ¼) for 40 minutes, or until the icing has set hard.

4. Add dots on either side of the flame with yellow line icing and add definition to the flame.

5. Outline the boat shape in orange line icing and add some wiggly lines across it in dark pink line icing.

6. Finish by using black line icing to pipe a tiny line for a candlewick. Allow to fully dry.

Teardrop

Line: yellow / dark red / white / blue
Flood: yellow

1. Use yellow line icing to draw a flowing teardrop shape on the biscuit. Leave to dry for 10 minutes at room temperature.

2. Once dry, flood with yellow flood icing.

3. Place the biscuit onto a baking tray and into an oven set to the lowest temperature (50°C/gas mark ¼) for 40 minutes, or until the icing has set hard.

4. Pipe your message onto the biscuit in dark red line icing.

5. Finally, pipe white and blue dots around the teardrop shape to finish the biscuit off. Allow to fully dry.

Orange flower

Line: orange / dark pink / black
Flood: orange / pink / blue

1. Using orange line icing, pipe around the edge of your flower biscuit and then pipe 2 circles in the middle. Leave to dry for 10 minutes at room temperature.

2. Once dry, flood the outer biscuit with orange flood icing, then the bigger circle with pink flood icing and the middle circle with blue flood icing.

3. Place the biscuit onto a baking tray and into an oven set to the lowest temperature (50°C/gas mark ¼) for 40 minutes, or until the icing has set hard.

4. Use dark pink line icing to pipe swirls onto each petal of the biscuit and then a flower shape in the middle of the blue circle.

5. Use blue line icing to add 3 dots next to each swirl and then pipe an outline around the pink circle.

6. Use orange line icing to pipe an outline round the blue circle and then lots of petals around it, finishing with a dot in the very centre of the flower. Allow to fully dry.

Halloween Ghost Bunting

Scarily simple and ghoulishly great, what could be better than party decorations you can eat? Ice one for each of your Halloween guests and dare them to eat it right off the ribbon … no hands allowed!

You will need:

1 batch of shaped biscuits* (recipes pp.19–25)

1 batch of Royal Icing (recipe p.30), divided into line and flood consistencies in the following colours:

Line: white
Flood: white / black

Ribbon or string

* Don't forget to cut a medium-sized hole towards the top of the biscuits, before baking, so you can thread your string through later. Use the end of a straw to cut out the perfect-sized hole from your uncooked dough!

1. Use white line icing to outline your ghost shape on the biscuits. Outline 2 eyes and a mouth and outline the cut-out hole, too. Leave to dry for 10 minutes at room temperature.

2. Once dry, fill in the eyes and mouth shapes with black flood icing, then flood the rest of the ghost with white flood icing.

3. Place the biscuits onto a baking tray and into an oven set to the lowest temperature (50°C/gas mark ¼) for 40 minutes, or until the icing has set hard.

4. Cut a long strip of string or ribbon and, using a toothpick, push the end through the hole in one of the biscuits. Tie the string in a knot and repeat with the next biscuit, until all the biscuits have been threaded.

Halloween Spider Cake

More treat than trick, this cake will wow your
guests, but involves just a few simple techniques.
The spiders can be served with the cake at
your Halloween party, or wrapped up and
put into your goody bags!

You will need:

3 x 20-cm/8-inch Red Velvet Cake layers (recipe p.28)

1 batch of Chocolate Buttercream (recipe p.35)

3 tbsp apricot jam

25-cm/10-inch cake board

1 batch of Royal Icing (recipe p.30)

Iced Spider Biscuits (see instructions opposite)

1. Bake your cakes according to the recipe. Once the
   cake layers are completely cool, you can stack them up.
   Using a sharp knife, carefully level the top of each
   layer – they will need to sit flat.

2. Smear a little buttercream onto the cake board and place
   the first cake layer on top, to secure it to the board.

3. Using a palette knife, spread the buttercream evenly over
   the top of the first layer, then place another cake layer
   on top. Repeat.

4. Put the apricot jam in the microwave for around 30 seconds,
   until it is slightly warm. Using a pastry brush, cover the cake
   with a thin layer of jam. Allow to cool completely.

5. Once cool, use white line icing to pipe a spider-web
   pattern all around the outside of your cake. Starting on
   the top of the cake, pipe a small circle in the centre, and
   then 8 lines coming out from the edge of the circle to the
   outer edge of the top of the cake (this will create 8 triangle
   segments on the top of the cake). In each segment, pipe
   lots of curved parallel lines. Once all the segments are filled,
   you will be left with a spider web shape. Repeat on the sides
   of the cake until completely covered.

6. Allow to dry. Decorate with Spider Biscuits, if you wish.

Spider Biscuits

1 batch of shaped biscuits (recipes pp.19–25)

1 batch of Royal Icing (recipe p.30), divided into line
and flood consistencies in the following colours:

Line: black / orange
Flood: black

1. Use black line icing to pipe around the outline of
   your spider biscuits. Leave to dry for 10 minutes at
   room temperature.

2. Once dry, flood your spider shapes with black flood icing.

3. Place the biscuits onto a baking tray and into an oven
   set to the lowest temperature (50°C/gas mark ¼) for
   40 minutes, or until the icing has set hard.

4. Outline the body, head and legs of the spiders with black
   line icing.

5. Finish off with two orange dots for eyes. Allow to fully dry.

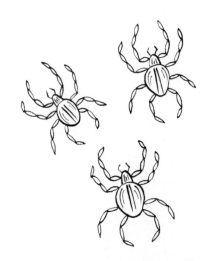

Piñata Biscuits

If you're a little more cool than ghoul, our
Mexican-inspired skulls will be right up your
street for Halloween or Day of the Dead.
Be as creative as you like with the icing
colours, and choose a sweet filling to match.

You will need:

1 batch of Chocolate Biscuit dough (recipe p.23)

1 batch of Royal Icing (recipe p.30), divided into line
and flood consistencies in the following colours:

*Line: grey / white / black / turquoise / lime green /
orange / pink*

Flood: orange / green / grey / black / yellow / white

Sweets and treats (mini chocolate beans, sprinkles,
mini candy corn), to fill

1. Line a baking tray with greaseproof paper. Preheat the
   oven to 150°C/130°C fan/gas 2.

2. Roll the biscuit dough out to a thickness of 6mm.

3. Choose a spooky biscuit cutter, such as a pumpkin,
   tombstone or skull, and cut 3 of each chosen shape
   from the dough. From one of the shapes, cut out
   the middle (this will form the secret 'compartment'
   for the sweets), then place your shapes on the pre-lined
   baking tray. You should have 2 x full biscuit shapes
   and 1 x 'frame' shape, for each piñata.

4. Bake in the hot oven for 20–25 minutes, depending on size.

5. Remove the tray from the oven and transfer the whole
   sheet of greaseproof paper to a cooling rack. Leave to
   completely cool, before starting to ice.

6. Use a line icing colour of your choice to ice around the
   edges of the biscuits and leave to dry for 10 minutes at
   room temperature. Remember, you only need to ice the
   top biscuits (half of your 'full' biscuit shapes).

7. Once dry, flood the biscuits with your chosen colour
   of flood icing.

8. Place the biscuits onto a baking tray and into an oven
   set to the lowest temperature (50°C/gas mark ¼) for
   40 minutes, or until the icing has set hard.

9. Finally, decorate the biscuits as you wish with line icing.
   You could ice creepy skeleton hands, tombstone markers,
   spooky pumpkins or Mexican skull designs.

10. Using line icing as 'glue', layer the 'cut out' biscuits on
    top of one of the un-iced whole biscuits. If you have
    asymmetrical biscuit shapes, make sure all the bits will
    match when they are sandwiched. Leave to dry for
    10 minutes.

11. Now, fill the gap with treats and sandwich the iced
    biscuit shapes on top, again using a little line icing as
    'glue'. Allow to fully dry.

Thanksgiving

The colour palette of this collection couldn't be more autumnal if we tried, and the pumpkin and turkey are straight out of an all-American Thanksgiving feast. There are plenty of techniques to get stuck into, including feathering, flood-on-flood and sanding sugar.

You will need:

1 batch of shaped biscuits (recipes pp.19–25)

1 batch of Royal Icing (recipe p.30), divided into line and flood consistencies (colours detailed in individual biscuit instructions)

Granulated sugar

Pumpkin

Line: orange / brown
Flood: orange

1. Use orange line icing to outline the first segment of your pumpkin to the left-hand side of the biscuit – the segments are banana-shaped!

2. Continue piping the rest of the pumpkin segments side-by-side. Leave to dry for 10 minutes at room temperature.

3. Once dry, flood each individual segment of the pumpkin with orange flood icing.

4. Place the biscuit onto a baking tray and into an oven set to the lowest temperature (50°C/gas mark ¼) for 40 minutes, or until the icing has set hard.

5. Use brown line icing to pipe in a back-and-forth motion at the top of the pumpkin to create the stalk. Allow to fully dry.

Leaf

Line: orange / red / brown / yellow
Flood: orange / brown / white / red / yellow

1. Outline your leaf biscuit with orange line icing. Leave to dry for 10 minutes at room temperature.

2. Once dry, use orange flood icing to pipe a thick line around the inside edge of the biscuit. Use brown flood to pipe a thick line inside the orange line. Fill in with white flood. Finally, in the centre, pipe a small dot of red flood icing.

3. While the icing is still wet, drag a cocktail stick several times through the wet icing from the centre to the outer edge. Wipe the cocktail stick clean between each drag.

4. Place the biscuit onto a baking tray and into an oven set to the lowest temperature (50°C/gas mark ¼) for 40 minutes, or until the icing has set hard.

TOP TIP – *Repeat with a variety of different autumnal colours, such as red, yellow and brown!*

Acorn

Line: beige / light green / brown / white
Flood: light green / beige

1. Using beige line icing, pipe the outline of the top section and the stalk of the acorn.

2. Use light green line icing to outline the bottom half of the acorn. Leave to dry for 10 minutes at room temperature.

3. Once dry, flood the bottom section with light green flood icing. While the icing is still wet, sprinkle with sugar and gently tap off any excess.

4. Flood the top section and stalk with beige flood icing.

5. Place the biscuit onto a baking tray and into an oven set to the lowest temperature (50°C/gas mark ¼) for 40 minutes, or until the icing has set hard.

6. Use brown line icing to pipe a grid pattern over the top beige section.

7. Finally, use white line icing to pipe a line down the side of the green section, to look like a reflection. Allow to fully dry.

Christmas Holiday

When the weather outside is frightful, the fire is so delightful! Just looking at this collection will give you warm feelings, as will icing it for your nearest and dearest. Let it snow, let it snow, let it snow…

You will need:

1 batch of shaped biscuits (recipes pp.19–25)

1 batch of Royal Icing (recipe p.30), divided into line and flood consistencies (colours detailed in individual biscuit instructions)

Edible gold ball decorations (for Front door biscuits)

Mittens

Line: cream / mint green / white

1. Start at the top of the mitten and, in a back-and-forth motion, pipe a line of cream line icing.

2. Directly underneath, repeat with a line of mint green line icing.

3. Repeat in alternate lines of colour until the mittens are full.

4. Along the bottom of each mitten use white line icing to pipe a thicker line of icing. Leave to dry for 10 minutes at room temperature.

Candy cane

Line: red
Flood: red / white

1. Outline your candy cane biscuit with red line icing. Then pipe diagonal stripes across the biscuit, all the way to the top. Leave to dry for 10 minutes at room temperature.

2. Once dry, use white flood icing to flood the bottom section. Then flood the section above with red flood icing.

3. Repeat, until all the segments are filled with alternate colours.

4. Place the biscuit onto a baking tray and into an oven set to the lowest temperature (50°C/gas mark ¼) for 40 minutes, or until the icing has set hard.

5. Use red line icing to pipe over the line between each section, adding definition to the candy cane. Allow to fully dry.

Front door with wreath

Line: red / white / green
Flood: red

1. Use red line icing to pipe the outline of the door. Leave to dry for 10 minutes at room temperature.

2. Once dry, flood the shape with red flood icing.

3. Place the biscuit onto a baking tray and into an oven set to the lowest temperature (50°C/gas mark ¼) for 40 minutes, or until the icing has set hard.

4. Use red line icing to pipe 2 squares side-by-side on the bottom third of the door. Above these squares, pipe 2 long rectangles.

5. In the space between the squares and rectangles, pipe a small dot. While the dot is wet, gently press an edible gold ball into the wet icing – this will be the door handle!

6. Use green line icing to pipe a ring near the top of the door. Leave to dry for 10 minutes.

7. Use white line icing to pipe a scatter of dots over the green ring, and a bow at the top. Allow to fully dry.

Advent

For us, Advent is one of the most exciting parts of the festive season. There is something so magical about hanging up a calendar and hiding a biscuit in each pocket, ready to count down to the big day, one biscuit at a time. We love puddings, snowy trees and presents wrapped with a bow, for a traditional feel.

You will need:

1 batch of shaped biscuits (recipes pp.19–25)

1 batch of Royal Icing (recipe p.30), divided into line and flood consistencies (colours detailed in individual biscuit instructions)

Granulated sugar (for the Christmas tree)

Christmas tree

Line: brown / icy blue / white

1. Ice the trunk of the tree onto the biscuit in brown line icing.

2. Using icy blue line icing, pipe 3 layers of vertical zig-zag lines on the biscuit, for branches. Allow to dry for a few minutes.

3. Using white line icing in a back-and-forth motion, pipe 3 layers of snow, one at the bottom of each layer of the tree.

4. While the icing is still wet, sprinkle sugar over for a sparkly effect. Tap off any excess.

5. Using white line icing, pipe a series of dots all over the tree to look like snowflakes on the branches.

6. Finally, use white line icing to pipe a star on the top of the tree. Allow to fully dry.

Christmas pudding

Line: brown / white / red / icy blue
Flood: brown / white

1. Use brown line icing to pipe around the bottom
   outer edge of a circular biscuit. Pipe a scalloped line
   horizontally across the centre.

2. Use white line icing to pipe the top outer edge of the
   biscuit. Leave to dry for 10 minutes at room temperature.

3. Once dry, flood the bottom section with brown flood
   icing and the top section with white flood icing.

4. Place the biscuit onto a baking tray and into an oven
   set to the lowest temperature (50°C/gas mark ¼) for
   40 minutes, or until the icing has set hard.

5. Pipe 2 rows of dots onto the brown section with red
   line icing.

6. At the top of the white section, pipe a cluster of 3 dots
   with red line icing. Then use icy blue line icing to pipe
   2 holly leaves. Allow to fully dry.

Present

Line: red / icy blue
Flood: red / white

1. Use red line icing to outline a square on your biscuit.
   Leave to dry for 10 minutes at room temperature.

2. Once dry, using red and white flood icings, pipe alternate
   thick stripes horizontally across the biscuit.

3. While the flood icing is still wet, drag a cocktail stick
   vertically through the wet icing in alternating directions,
   several times. Wipe the cocktail stick clean between
   each drag.

4. Place the biscuit onto a baking tray and into an oven
   set to the lowest temperature (50°C/gas mark ¼) for
   40 minutes, or until the icing has set hard.

5. Finally, use icy blue line icing to pipe a bow onto the
   present. Allow to fully dry.

Christmas Cake

We take Christmas-cake making very seriously at Biscuiteers.
For the best taste, your fruit cake should be left for three months
to mature. To keep it beautifully moist, brush it with brandy
every four to six weeks. Once you're ready to cover your cake,
our festive wreath design is very simple to achieve with line icing.

You will need:

1 x 20-cm/8-inch Mature Fruit Cake (recipe p.29)

3 tbsp apricot jam or marmalade

25-cm/10-inch cake board

Icing sugar, for dusting

700g marzipan

700g white fondant icing (shop-bought, room temperature)

Icy blue food colouring (gel or paste, NOT liquid)

Pearl shimmer dust

Thick, natural cake ribbon (80cm)

1 batch of Royal Icing (recipe p.30), line consistency,
in the following colours:

white / brown / beige / green / icy blue / red

1. Measure across the top and sides of your cake using a
   piece of string or cotton – this will act as a guide for rolling
   out your marzipan and fondant. Cut to size and set aside.

2. Place the jam or marmalade in a small saucepan with
   2 teaspoons of water. Warm over a low heat until runny.

3. Use a pastry brush to apply a little warm jam to the cake
   board, then secure the cake to the board. Generously
   brush the cake with the rest of the mixture and set aside.

4. Sprinkle a little icing sugar onto a clean work surface.
   Roll the marzipan into a ball and flatten into a disc shape.
   Roll out the marzipan to an even thickness, about 5mm,
   with a rolling pin. Use your piece of string to check that
   your marzipan is big enough to cover your cake.

5. Lift the marzipan and smooth it over the cake, using
   a fondant smoother to smooth down the top and sides.
   Cut off any excess, tucking the bottom edges of the
   marzipan underneath the cake.

6. Place the cake in a tin or cover with baking parchment
   for at least 24 hours, to allow the marzipan to dry.

7. Clear a large, smooth work surface so that it is clean
   and free of crumbs – imperfections will be visible on the
   fondant. Dust the surface generously with icing sugar.
   Knead the fondant for 2 minutes, or until softened.

8. Add a small amount of food colouring to the fondant,
   and knead it until an even colour develops. Roll the
   fondant into a ball, then flatten it into a round disc shape.

9. Lightly brush the marzipan-covered cake with freshly
   boiled water – this will help the fondant icing to stick.

10. Lightly dust a rolling pin with icing sugar. Roll out the
    fondant until it is about 5mm thick, giving it a quarter
    turn now and then, to keep it even and round. Use the
    measured string as a guide – the fondant should be slightly
    bigger than the string. You can trim excess fondant later.

11. Loosely drape the fondant over the rolling pin, then lift
    and roll it up and over the cake. Smooth the surface with
    a fondant smoother or a smooth glass. Start on the top
    and then move down the sides. Be careful to avoid folds,
    wrinkles and air bubbles. If any bubbles develop, pop them
    with a pin, then smooth over with the fondant smoother.

12. Once the fondant is smooth, use a small knife or pizza
    cutter to cut away any excess at the bottom of the cake.
    Try to cut as close to the bottom of the cake as possible.

13. With a clean paintbrush, brush a layer of shimmer dust
    over the cake.

14. Cut the cake ribbon to size, wrap around the bottom
    of the cake and secure with a blob of white line icing.

15. Now for the fun bit! Use brown and beige line icing to
    pipe lots of large rings around the top of the cake.
    Use white line icing to pipe dots, for frosty berries.
    Use green and icy blue line icing to pipe holly leaves
    scattered around the wreath. Leave to dry for 10 minutes.

16. When dry, pipe the veins of the holly leaves with icy blue
    or white line icing and, finally, add some berries with red
    line icing. Allow to fully dry.

Nutcracker

Take your seat at the biscuit ballet, our *Nutcracker*
production has begun! Ice your very own cast
of enchanting ballet dancers, and be the guest
of honour at the dance of the Sugar Plum Fairy.

You will need:

1 batch of shaped biscuits (recipes pp.19–25)

1 batch of Royal Icing (recipe p.30), divided into line
and flood consistencies (colours detailed in individual
biscuit instructions)

Granulated sugar

Edible gold paint

Gold sweet

Line: white / beige

1. Use white line icing to pipe a large, tight swirl in the
   middle of your biscuit.

2. While the icing is still wet, sprinkle sugar over the top.
   Gently tap off any excess.

3. Pipe 4 thick lines either side of the circle in beige line
   icing to give the effect of a wrapper.

4. On top of your sugary white swirl, pipe dots of beige
   line icing all over. Leave to dry for 10 minutes at
   room temperature.

5. Using a clean paintbrush and edible gold paint, paint each
   dot so they look super shiny and golden. Allow to dry.

Nutcracker

Line: black / ivory / red
Flood: black / ivory / red

1. Pipe the outline of the hat on the biscuit in black line
   icing. Underneath, draw a square shape for the face
   in ivory line icing. Pipe the nutcracker's body, nipped in
   at the waist, and arms with red line icing and use the ivory
   line icing to pipe 2 legs. Finally, pipe 2 boots in black line
   icing. Leave to dry for 10 minutes at room temperature.

2. Fill the hat and boots with black flood icing, the face and
   legs with ivory flood and the body and arms with red
   flood. You'll need to use squeezy bottles with smaller tips
   for this, as the biscuit is very detailed.

3. Place the biscuit onto a baking tray and into an oven
   set to the lowest temperature (50°C/gas mark ¼) for
   40 minutes, or until the icing has set hard.

4. Use ivory line icing to pipe a trim on the hat, epaulettes,
   buttons and cuffs, and a line at the top of each boot.

5. Use white line icing to pipe his beard, hair and eyes, and
   black for his belt, eyebrows, pupils, moustache and mouth.

6. Finish the biscuit by painting gold edible paint carefully
   onto the trim details. Allow to fully dry.

Sugar plum fairy

Line: ivory / white / black / beige
Flood: ivory

1. Outline the face, arms, body and legs on your biscuit
   in ivory line icing. We've left a small gap between the
   legs, but this is optional. Leave to dry for 10 minutes
   at room temperature.

2. Once dry, fill the face, arms, body and legs with
   ivory flood.

3. Place the biscuit onto a baking tray and into an oven
   set to the lowest temperature (50°C/gas mark ¼) for
   40 minutes, or until the icing has set hard.

4. Use white line icing to pipe a tutu between the body
   and the legs and add small white dots to the bodice.

5. Ice some hair in a ballerina bun with black line icing.

6. Give your ballerina some shoes and criss-cross
   ribbons in beige line icing. Leave to dry for 10 minutes.

7. Carefully paint gold metallic paint over the ballet shoes,
   to finish. Allow to fully dry.

Christmas Tree Decorations

A Biscuiteer's tree is never fully dressed without a collection of shimmering bauble biscuits and we look forward to the ritual of decorating the tree every year. Remember to cut the ribbon hole before you bake the biscuits and find a delicate craft brush to paint on the metallic shimmers.

You will need:

1 batch of shaped biscuits* (recipes pp.19–25)

1 batch of Royal Icing (recipe p.30), divided into line and flood consistencies (colours detailed in individual biscuit instructions)

Edible metallic paints in white, blue and gold

Ribbon

* Don't forget to cut a medium-sized hole towards the top of the biscuits, before baking, so you can thread your ribbons through later. Use the end of a straw to cut out the perfect-sized hole from your uncooked dough!

Blue large teardrop bauble

Line: blue / beige / white
Flood: blue

1. Use blue line icing to outline a wide teardrop shape on your biscuit and pipe around the cut-out hole. Use beige line icing to pipe the top of the bauble. Leave to dry for 10 minutes at room temperature.

2. Once dry, flood the teardrop with blue flood icing.

3. Place the biscuit onto a baking tray and into an oven set to the lowest temperature (50°C/gas mark ¼) for 40 minutes, or until the icing has set hard.

4. Use clean paintbrushes to brush blue edible metallic paint all over the blue icing and gold paint over the beige icing – a little bit goes a long way, so start off sparingly. Leave to dry for 10 minutes.

5. Use white line icing to pipe a star in the middle of the biscuit, then use a combination of white and beige line icing to add dots, lines and swirls. Allow to fully dry.

White bauble

Line: white / light pink / beige / light blue
Flood: white

1. Use white line icing to outline a circle on your biscuit and pipe around the cut-out hole. Use light pink line icing to pipe the top of the bauble. Leave to dry for 10 minutes at room temperature.

2. Once dry, flood the circle with white flood icing.

3. Place the biscuit onto a baking tray and into an oven set to the lowest temperature (50°C/gas mark ¼) for 40 minutes, or until the icing has set hard.

4. Use a clean paintbrush to brush white edible metallic paint all over the white icing. Leave to dry for 10 minutes.

5. Using beige line icing, pipe diagonal lines across the bauble, first one way and then the other. Pipe light blue dots in each diamond shape. Allow to fully dry.

Green small teardrop bauble

Line: turquoise / light pink / beige / light green
Flood: turquoise

1. Use turquoise line icing to outline a small teardrop shape on your biscuit and pipe around the cut-out hole. Use light pink line icing to pipe the top of the bauble. Leave to dry for 10 minutes at room temperature.

2. Once dry, flood the teardrop with turquoise flood icing.

3. Place the biscuit onto a baking tray and into an oven set to the lowest temperature (50°C/gas mark ¼) for 40 minutes, or until the icing has set hard.

4. Use beige line icing to pipe 5 curved lines on the left-hand side of the biscuit.

5. Along the first line pipe a series of light green dots, then along the second line pipe light pink dots. Repeat, alternating colours until you've done all of the lines. Allow to fully dry.

Christmas Biscuit Wreath

Inspired by the beautiful wreaths that decorate front doors at Christmas time, our biscuit version is sturdy enough to be hung. We've brushed metallic silver paint onto crisp snowflakes, but green holly and red berries would be just as festive. Lay flat in a gift box and tie with a red ribbon to gift to your favourite neighbour.

You will need:

1 batch of shaped snowflake biscuits (recipes pp.19–25)

1 batch of Royal Icing (recipe p.30), divided into line and flood consistencies in the following colours:

Line: white / grey

Flood: white / grey

Granulated sugar

Edible silver metallic paint

1 batch of All-Spice Biscuit dough (recipe p.20)

Thick ribbon

Snowflake biscuits

Ice your biscuit snowflakes in a variety of sizes, shapes, designs and patterns.

Option 1: Use line icing to pipe a snowflake pattern directly onto a plain biscuit base. Allow to dry.

Option 2: Outline your snowflake with your chosen colour of line icing. Leave to dry for 10 minutes. When dry, flood the snowflake with your chosen colour of flood icing. Place the biscuit onto a baking tray and into an oven set to the lowest temperature (50°C/gas mark ¼) for 40 minutes, or until the icing has set hard. When dry, pipe a snowflake pattern on top in line icing. While the line icing is still wet, sprinkle with sugar and then gently tap off any excess. Allow to fully dry.

Option 3: Create your snowflake with line and flood as in option 2. Once it has dried in the oven, use a clean paintbrush to paint the biscuit with edible metallic paint. Leave to dry for 10 minutes, then pipe a snowflake pattern on top with line icing. Allow to fully dry.

For the wreath

1. Preheat oven to 150°C/130°C fan/gas mark 2.

2. Place the biscuit dough between 2 sheets of greaseproof paper, then flatten the dough into a disc. Use a rolling pin to roll the dough out to an even thickness of about 1cm, then remove the top layer of greaseproof paper.

3. Using a ring-shaped paper template (our template is 30cm in diameter and 3cm wide), cut out a large circular shape, then cut out the middle to create a large ring of dough.

   TOP TIP – *To avoid your cutter or knife sticking to the dough, coat it in flour.*

4. Lift the bottom layer of paper with the dough ring on it and transfer it to a baking tray. Bake in the hot oven for 20–30 minutes, or until the biscuit is golden brown.

5. Remove from the oven and carefully transfer the sheet of greaseproof paper with the biscuit ring on it to a cooling rack. Allow the biscuit to completely cool.

6. Once your snowflake biscuits are decorated (see opposite) and the large ring has cooled, you can assemble your wreath.

7. Pipe a small amount of line icing onto the back of each snowflake biscuit and arrange them on your biscuit ring. We attached our larger snowflakes first and then filled in the gaps with the smaller ones.

8. Once all your biscuit snowflakes are attached to the base ring and you are happy with the arrangement, leave the wreath to dry for at least 1 hour.

9. As a finishing touch, take a piece of thick ribbon and loop it through the middle of your wreath, tying it in a bow at the top.

Gingerbread House

A great project for the whole family to get stuck into on Christmas Eve. Why not attempt a whole gingerbread village if you have aunties, uncles and cousins visiting?

You will need:

1 batch of All-Spice Biscuit dough (recipe p.20)

Royal Icing (recipe p.30), white or coloured as you wish

Edible decorations and sprinkles of your choice

Cake board

1. Draw out a template for your gingerbread house. You can make the house as large or small as you like, but here are the basics for working out the dimensions:

   On a sheet of paper, use a pencil and ruler to mark out 2 long slim rectangles (sides of the house), 2 wider rectangles of the same length (roof of the house) and 2 squares that come up to a triangle point (ends of the house). The width of the squares should be the same as the short sides of your side pieces and the apex of the triangle should meet where 2 sides of the same width as your roof pieces meet. Cut out your paper templates with scissors and set to one side.

2. Line a baking tray with greaseproof paper. Preheat oven to 150°C/130° fan/gas mark 2.

3. Place the biscuit dough between 2 sheets of greaseproof paper, then flatten the dough into a disc.

4. Using a rolling pin, roll the dough out to an even thickness of about 1cm.

5. Remove the top layer of greaseproof paper. Lay your templates onto the dough and, using a sharp knife, carefully cut around each template (leftover dough can be used to make Christmas trees or something else to decorate the house!).

6. Use a palette knife to lift and transfer the cut-out dough shapes to the lined baking tray. Bake in the hot oven for 20–30 minutes, or until the biscuits look golden brown.

7. Remove from the oven and carefully transfer the sheet of greaseproof paper with the biscuits on it to a cooling rack. Allow the biscuits to cool.

8. When your biscuits are completely cool, it's time to decorate and assemble your house. It's best to decorate the house before assembly, so that the decorations can dry flat.

   TOP TIP – *Draw your decorative design onto paper before you start icing onto the biscuits.*

9. Use line icing to pipe decorative roof tiles, window panes and snowflakes. Leave to dry for 30 minutes. To stick decorations to the house, pipe a small dot of line icing to the back of the decoration and gently press it onto the biscuit.

10. Once your decorated pieces are dry, you are ready to put the house together. To start, pipe a thick line of line icing along the bottom and edges of the front piece, do the same for both the side pieces. Stick them together, on the cake board base, and hold for a few minutes, until the pieces feel set. They will take about 15 minutes to fully set, so prop them up with some glasses or mugs, to hold them steady while they dry.

11. Pipe a thick line of icing along the bottom of the back piece and along the edges of the side pieces, then attach the back piece to the cake board and back edges of the house. Allow to set as before.

12. To assemble the roof, you need to pipe a line of icing along the top edges of the house, then stick the roof pieces to the top of the house. They will need to be assembled one at a time and held in place for 10–15 minutes, so the icing has time to set.

13. To finish, ice the space in-between the two roof pieces at the top of the house. Allow to fully set.

14. If wished, you can also cut out, bake and decorate a chimney to stick to the top of the roof. You will need to cut out 4 rectangles, then cut 2 triangle shapes out of the bottom of 2 of them. Stick together as above, then stick to the top of your house, icing around the base to cover the join.

Christmas Jolly Gingers

Every stocking deserves
a Biscuiteers Jolly Ginger!

You will need:

1 batch of shaped All-Spice Biscuits (recipe p.20)

1 batch of Royal Icing (recipe p.30), line consistency,
in the following colours:

**brown / purple / white / grey / red / green /
beige / black / blue**

Edible silver metallic paint

Ice skater

1. Outline the boots on your jolly ginger in brown line icing.

2. Then, using purple line icing, pipe the outline of a jumper.
   Add little vertical lines at the bottom edge and neck of
   the jumper.

3. With white line icing, pipe mittens, a snowflake on
   the jumper and a bobble hat.

4. Pipe a smiley face and some hair coming out of the
   hat in brown line icing. Leave to dry for 10 minutes
   at room temperature.

5. Pipe 2 grey lines by the shoulders to make the laces for
   the boots. Then use white line icing to pipe 2 skating boot
   shapes. Use the grey line icing again to pipe laces on the
   boots and the blades of the ice skates.

6. Finally, use a clean paintbrush to paint edible silver metallic
   paint on the blades of the boots to make them look shiny.
   Allow to fully dry.

Elf

1. Outline and fill in the boots and collar on your jolly ginger
   in red line icing.

2. Then, outline the shape of the elf in green line icing.
   Don't forget to add stripes for the socks and a zig-zag
   to define the top of the trousers.

3. In the middle of the jolly ginger pipe a thick brown
   line for the belt, then pipe a belt buckle on top in
   beige line icing.

4. With brown line icing, pipe a smiley mouth and eyes.
   Pipe 2 red dots either side of the mouth to give the elf
   rosy cheeks.

5. Above the eyes pipe a line in red line icing. Then, using
   green line icing, pipe a droopy elf hat.

6. Finish by icing a bell at the end of the hat in beige line
   icing. Allow to fully dry.

Carol singer

1. Pipe 2 eyes on your jolly ginger with brown line icing,
   then pipe an open mouth, as though the jolly ginger
   is singing.

2. Use black line icing to pipe a line over the top of the head,
   then pipe 2 circles with blue to make the ear muffs.

3. Pipe a blue scarf shape with tassels, then, using red line
   icing, pipe on some stripes.

4. Give your jolly ginger some arms in brown line icing,
   then pipe 2 mittens in blue line icing. Don't forget to
   fill the mittens in with the blue icing, using a back-and-
   forth motion.

5. To create the book, pipe 2 jaunty rectangles and fill
   in with green line icing. Then, add 2 white lines in
   a wide V shape at the top and finally a musical note,
   also in white. Be careful not to ice over the mittens!
   Allow to fully dry.

Thank You

We love making biscuits for all kinds of people and occasions, but often find ourselves back at 'Thank You'. The most rewarding present to give, and perhaps the most unexpected. We like to spell it out with lettering, iced in bold colours and patterns. Letter cutters are easy to find online.

You will need:

1 batch of shaped biscuits (recipes pp.19–25)

1 batch of Royal Icing (recipe p.30), divided into line and flood consistencies (colours detailed in individual biscuit instructions)

Thank you

Line: dark pink
Flood: dark pink / yellow / blue

1. Using dark pink line icing, pipe around the outline of your Thank you biscuits. Leave to dry for 10 minutes at room temperature.

2. Once dry, fill your biscuits with dark pink flood icing.

3. While the icing is still wet, randomly pipe dots of yellow and blue flood icing directly into the pink flood.

4. Place the biscuits onto a baking tray and into an oven set to the lowest temperature (50°C/gas mark ¼) for 40 minutes, or until the icing has set hard.

Merci

Line: white
Flood: white / pink / orange

1. Using white line icing, pipe around the outline of your Merci biscuits. Leave to dry for 10 minutes at room temperature.

2. Once dry, fill your biscuits with white flood icing.

3. While the icing is still wet, using pink and orange flood icing, pipe alternate horizontal stripes across the biscuits.

4. Using a cocktail stick, starting at the top of each letter, drag the stick down through the icing to the bottom of each biscuit and repeat in the alternate direction (wiping the cocktail stick clean between each drag). This icing technique is called 'feathering'.

5. Place the biscuits onto a baking tray and into an oven set to the lowest temperature (50°C/gas mark ¼) for 40 minutes, or until the icing has set hard.

Gracias

Line: blue / hot pink / light pink
Flood: blue

1. Using blue line icing, pipe around the outline of your Gracias biscuits. Leave to dry for 10 minutes at room temperature.

2. Once dry, fill your biscuits with blue flood icing.

3. While the icing is still wet, using hot pink and light pink line icing, pipe alternate stripes vertically down the biscuits.

4. Place the biscuits onto a baking tray and into an oven set to the lowest temperature (50°C/gas mark ¼) for 40 minutes, or until the icing has set hard.

Get Well Fruit Basket

Guaranteed to raise a smile from a friend with the sniffles or a bad case of the blues, there's no better way to say 'Get well soon.' Sometimes a bunch of grapes just won't do!

You will need:

1 batch of shaped biscuits (recipes pp.19–25)

1 batch of Royal Icing (recipe p.30), divided into line and flood consistencies (colours detailed in individual biscuit instructions)

Lemon or Orange

Line: yellow or orange / white
Flood: yellow or orange / cream

1. Pipe the outline of a circle or semi-circle on your biscuit using yellow or orange line icing. Leave to dry for 10 minutes at room temperature.

2. Once dry, fill the centre of the shape with yellow or orange flood icing, leaving a small gap around the edge. Fill this outer gap with cream coloured flood icing.

3. Using a cocktail stick, gently drag small lines of the cream flood into the yellow or orange flood – you want to do this about 10 times, spaced around the biscuit (wipe the cocktail stick clean between each drag).

4. Place the biscuit onto a baking tray and into an oven set to the lowest temperature (50°C/gas mark ¼) for 40 minutes, or until the icing has set hard.

5. With yellow or orange line icing, pipe small wiggles across the biscuit. Then, using white line icing, pipe small teardrop shapes in the centre to create the pips. Allow to fully dry.

Kiwi

Line: lime green / brown / black
Flood: lime green / cream

1. Pipe the outline of a circle on your biscuit with lime green line icing. Leave to dry for 10 minutes at room temperature.

2. Once dry, flood the whole circle with lime green flood icing – be careful not to over-fill!

3. When the icing is still wet, pipe a good-sized circle of cream flood icing into the middle of the circle.

4. Using a cocktail stick, and with a back-and-forth motion, drag the stick through the outer edge of the cream flood so that it mixes into the lime green flood slightly.

5. Place the biscuit onto a baking tray and into an oven set to the lowest temperature (50°C/gas mark ¼) for 40 minutes, or until the icing has set hard.

6. Using brown line icing, pipe a circle round the outer edge of the circle, to create the skin of the kiwi. Then, with black line icing, add lots of dots around the centre to look like the kiwi seeds. Allow to fully dry.

Watermelon

Line: green / hot pink / lime green / black
Flood: green / hot pink

1. Using green line icing, pipe the outline of an arch shape at the edge of a semi-circular biscuit. Then pipe the inner flat edge of the biscuit with hot pink line icing. Leave to dry for 10 minutes at room temperature.

2. Once dry, flood the skin of the watermelon (the arch shape) with green flood icing, and then the main semi-circular section with hot pink flood icing.

3. Place the biscuit onto a baking tray and into an oven set to the lowest temperature (50°C/gas mark ¼) for 40 minutes, or until the icing has set hard.

4. Use lime green line icing to pipe a line on the inner edge of the green arch.

5. Finally, use black line icing to add two curved rows of teardrop-shaped dots to look like watermelon seeds. Allow to fully dry.

Get Well Soon

New Baby

The sweetest collection to celebrate a baby shower, welcome a new arrival into the world or toast a christening. Choose your icing colours for a baby boy or girl, and ice their name onto the babygrow.

You will need:

1 batch of shaped biscuits (recipes pp.19–25)

1 batch of Royal Icing (recipe p.30), divided into line and flood consistencies (colours detailed in individual biscuit instructions)

Edible silver metallic paint

Silver spoon

Line: grey / white
Flood: grey

1. Pipe the outline of a spoon on the biscuit with grey line icing. Allow to dry for 10 minutes at room temperature.

2. Once dry, flood the spoon shape with grey flood icing.

3. Place the biscuit onto a baking tray and into an oven set to the lowest temperature (50°C/gas mark ¼) for 40 minutes, or until the icing has set hard.

4. Using white line icing, outline the oval at the top of the spoon, and then pipe a curved line to look like reflected light. At this stage, you can also add detail to the handle of the spoon, such as more reflections and a small crown. Allow to dry for 10 minutes.

5. Dip a clean paintbrush into the edible silver paint and paint the surface of the piped oval and crown. Allow to fully dry.

Babygrow

Line: cream
Flood: olive / cream

1. Use cream line icing to pipe the outline of the babygrow on the biscuit. At the neck of the babygrow pipe 2 scallop shapes. Leave to dry for 10 minutes at room temperature.

2. Once dry, flood the scalloped shapes at the neck with olive flood icing – be careful not to over-fill. Flood the rest of the babygrow with cream flood icing.

3. Place the biscuit onto a baking tray and into an oven set to the lowest temperature (50°C/gas mark ¼) for 40 minutes, or until the icing has set hard.

4. Use cream line icing to outline the scallops at the neck of the baby grow. Pipe a couple of dots at the bottom of the babygrow, on either shoulder and a row of 5 down the centre. Leave to dry for 10 minutes.

5. Dip a clean paintbrush into the edible silver paint and paint the surface of each piped dot. Allow to fully dry.

Rattle

Line: olive / cream
Flood: olive / cream

1. Use olive line icing to pipe a circle shape for the top of the rattle and a ring shape at the bottom of the biscuit.

2. Use cream line icing to pipe 2 lines for a handle to join the circle and ring together. Leave to dry for 10 minutes at room temperature.

3. Once dry, flood the circle and ring with olive flood icing.

4. Flood the handle with cream flood icing.

5. Place the biscuit onto a baking tray and into an oven set to the lowest temperature (50°C/gas mark ¼) for 40 minutes, or until the icing has set hard.

6. Use cream line icing to pipe small dots around the edge of the circle, 3 hearts across the centre and lines of decorative detail.

7. Use olive line icing to pipe a bow across the handle of the rattle. Allow to fully dry.

New Home

A townhouse with a red door, or a rose-covered cottage – we love icing our friend's new homes in biscuit form to celebrate moving-in day. Remember the all-important door number and a shiny gold key!

You will need:

1 batch of shaped biscuits (recipes pp.19–25)

1 batch of Royal Icing (recipe p.30), divided into line and flood consistencies (colours detailed in individual biscuit instructions)

Edible gold shimmer paint

Gold key

Line: beige
Flood: beige

1. Pipe the outline of a key shape on your biscuit with beige line icing. Leave to dry for 10 minutes at room temperature.

2. Once dry, flood the shape with beige flood icing.

3. Place the biscuit onto a baking tray and into an oven set to the lowest temperature (50°C/gas mark ¼) for 40 minutes, or until the icing has set hard.

4. Use beige line icing to pipe back around the outline of the key and add decorative details at the top. Leave to dry for 10 minutes.

5. Finally, using a clean paint brush, carefully paint over the surface of the icing with edible gold paint. Allow to dry.

Yellow townhouse

Line: white / red
Flood: yellow

1. Use white line icing to pipe the outline of the house on your biscuit, including the windows and front door.

Leave space for the roof. Leave to dry for 10 minutes at room temperature.

2. When dry, flood the house with yellow flood icing. Be careful not to flood the windows or door!

3. Place the biscuit onto a baking tray and into an oven set to the lowest temperature (50°C/gas mark ¼) for 40 minutes, or until the icing has set hard.

4. Using red line icing, pipe in a back-and-forth motion until the roof of the house is covered.

5. Outline the windows, door and panels of the house with white line icing. Finally, pipe 2 dots on top of the roof for finials, and a horizontal line to define the base of the roof. Allow to fully dry.

Bunch of flowers

Line: white / green / yellow / red
Flood: white

1. Using white line icing, pipe an upside-down triangle shape for the bottom of the bouquet on the biscuit. Leave to dry for 10 minutes at room temperature.

2. When dry, flood the shape with white flood icing.

3. Place the biscuit onto a baking tray and into an oven set to the lowest temperature (50°C/gas mark ¼) for 40 minutes, or until the icing has set hard.

4. Use green line icing to pipe leaves, yellow line icing to add small dots amongst the leaves and small swirls of red line icing to look like roses. Allow to fully dry.

How to Frame Biscuits

We might be biased, but we happen to think
that biscuits decorated by hand are works of art.
For very special occasions (to welcome a new baby,
to mark a milestone birthday or to celebrate a
wedding), we love to frame our biscuits to give
as thoughtful gifts. You can use any design of
biscuits in your frame. We've used butterflies
to look like vintage taxidermy displays.

You will need:

Box photo frame (you can buy these online
or at your local craft shop)

Thick white card

Royal icing (see p.30)

Iced biscuits of your choice

1. Measure the height and width of your frame, mark it
   out on the thick white card and carefully cut to size.

2. Place your selection of biscuits onto the card and
   find your ideal arrangement.

3. Use the royal icing to stick your biscuits to the card.
   The icing will act as a strong glue and, once dry, will
   keep the biscuits attached to the card in the frame.
   Gently pipe the icing directly onto the back of the
   biscuits, then carefully press the biscuits onto the card
   in the correct positions.

4. Leave to dry for about 1 hour at room temperature,
   until the icing has completely set.

5. Carefully place the display card into your frame, and
   that's it! You are ready to give someone special their
   handmade gift.

Love Letters

Signed, sealed and delivered … there's no better way to say 'I'm yours' than with our love letter collection. Complete with air-mail stripes for those long-distance love affairs. Learn how to write in icing on p.38 and upgrade the message to a declaration of love.

You will need:

1 batch of shaped biscuits (recipes pp.19–25)

1 batch of Royal Icing (recipe p.30), divided into line and flood consistencies (colours detailed in individual biscuit instructions)

Edible gold metallic paint

Letter box

Line: red / black / white
Flood: red / black

1. Using red line icing, pipe the outline of the top of the letter box on your biscuit and the outline of the base in black line icing. Don't forget to ice a line in between to create 2 sections. Dry for 10 minutes at room temperature.

2. Once dry, flood the top section with red flood icing and the base with black flood.

3. Place the biscuits onto a baking tray and into an oven set to the lowest temperature (50°C/gas mark ¼) for 40 minutes, or until the icing has set hard.

4. Use red, black and white line icings to add your details: the letter-box slot, the mouldings and a white heart. Allow to fully dry.

Letter

Line: cream / blue / red / black
Flood: cream

1. Using cream line icing, pipe a rectangle around your biscuit. Leave to dry for 10 minutes at room temperature.

2. Once dry, flood with cream flood icing.

3. Place the biscuits onto a baking tray and into an oven set to the lowest temperature (50°C/gas mark ¼) for 40 minutes, or until the icing has set hard.

4. Pipe a double line of cream line icing all around the rectangle to form a narrow frame and then pipe alternate short lines of blue and red line icing within the frame, all the way around. Leave to dry for a few minutes.

5. Use black line icing to ice your message onto the biscuit.

6. You can add a stamp by piping some wiggly lines and an outline of a black heart, then fill the heart in with red line icing. Pipe a cream 'postal mark' below the stamp. Allow to dry for 10 minutes.

7. Dip a clean paintbrush into the edible gold paint and paint the 'postal mark'. Allow to fully dry.

Love bird

Line: white / cream / black / red
Flood: white / cream

1. Using white line icing, pipe the outline of the bird, then a little cream line icing square for the envelope. Leave to dry for 10 minutes at room temperature.

2. Once dry, fill the bird in with white flood icing and the envelope with cream flood icing.

3. Place the biscuits onto a baking tray and into an oven set to the lowest temperature (50°C/gas mark ¼) for 40 minutes, or until the icing has set hard.

4. Using white line icing, add the details on the bird's wings. You'll also need a dot of black line icing for the eye and a cream triangle for the beak.

5. Use cream line icing to create the envelope folds and, finally, pipe a small heart with red line icing in the middle. Allow to dry for 10 minutes.

6. Dip a clean paintbrush into the edible gold paint and paint the bird's beak. Allow to fully dry.

Traditional Hearts

Leave them in no doubt of your feelings with our intricate love hearts. To make them extra special, we've used gold shimmer paint, which you can apply (carefully!) using a craft paint brush. Who said romance was dead?

You will need:

1 batch of heart-shaped biscuits (recipes pp.19–25)

1 batch of Royal Icing (recipe p.30), divided into line and flood consistencies (colours detailed in individual biscuit instructions

Edible gold shimmer paint

Pastel-pink heart

Line: light pink / white
Flood: light pink

1. Using light-pink line icing, pipe the outline of your heart. Leave to dry for 10 minutes at room temperature.

2. Once dry, flood the shape with light pink flood icing.

3. Place the biscuit onto a baking tray and into an oven set to the lowest temperature (50°C/gas mark ¼) for 40 minutes, or until the icing has set hard.

4. Use white line icing to add swirls to one side of the heart. Leave to dry for 10 minutes.

5. Using a small clean brush, carefully brush a little edible gold shimmer paint over the designs. Allow to fully dry.

Golden heart

Line: cream / beige / white
Flood: cream

1. Using cream line icing, pipe the outline of your heart. Leave to dry for 10 minutes at room temperature.

2. Once dry, flood the shape with cream flood icing.

3. Place the biscuit onto a baking tray and into an oven set to the lowest temperature (50°C/gas mark ¼) for 40 minutes, or until the icing has set hard.

4. Using a small clean brush, gently paint the edible gold shimmer paint over the top of the icing. Leave to dry for 30 minutes.

5. Use cream line icing to pipe a line from the bottom tip of the heart curving up to the top, ending in a small circle of icing. Add leaf-like swirls on either side of the line. Repeat this on the opposite side.

6. In the top centre of the heart, carefully pipe another small heart with your cream line icing. Allow to fully dry.

Brooch-detail heart

Line: hot pink / beige / white
Flood: bubble-gum pink

1. Using hot pink line icing, pipe the outline of your heart. Leave to dry for 10 minutes at room temperature.

2. Once dry, flood the centre of the heart with bubble-gum pink flood icing.

3. Place the biscuit onto a baking tray and into an oven set to the lowest temperature (50°C/gas mark ¼) for 40 minutes, or until the icing has set hard.

4. Using beige line icing, pipe around the edge of the heart, to create a thin 'frame'.

5. Use white line icing to pipe a small oval in the centre of your heart. Leave this to dry for 10 minutes.

6. Once dry, use beige line icing to pipe small loops around the edge of the oval, and finish with a small heart at the centre. Allow to fully dry.

TOP TIP – *We've also made this cake for christenings and baby showers, with baby blue and pink birds. To really shake things up, ice the birds in tropical colours for a carnival-themed birthday.*

Valentine's Love-Bird Cake

Guaranteed to set hearts racing, our love-bird biscuits look picture perfect perched on top of a luxurious red velvet cake. A true labour of love for your heart's desire.

You will need:

3 x 20-cm/8-inch Red Velvet Cake layers (recipe p.28)

1 batch of Cream Cheese Icing (recipe p.35)

25-cm/10-inch cake board

Cake crumbs and decorative sprinkles, to decorate

2 Love-Bird Biscuits (see opposite)

1. Bake your cakes according to the recipe. Once the layers are completely cool, you can begin to stack them up. Using a sharp knife, carefully level the top of each cake layer so they sit flat.
2. Smear a little cream cheese icing onto the cake board and place the first cake layer on top, to secure it to the board.
3. Using a palette knife, spread the cream cheese icing evenly over the top of the first layer, then place another cake layer on top. Repeat.
4. Apply a generous layer of cream cheese icing to the top of the cake and, using a back-and-forth motion with your palette knife, smooth the icing across the top of the cake and down the sides, until it is covered in an even layer of icing.
5. Take some leftover cake crumbs or sprinkles and add a scattering to the top of the cake. Carefully insert the Love-Bird Biscuits into your cake so that they mirror each other.

Love-Bird Biscuits

1 batch of shaped biscuits (recipes pp.19–25)

1 batch of Royal Icing (recipe p.30), divided into line and flood consistencies in the following colours:

Line: hot pink / black / baby pink / white
Flood: hot pink / baby pink / white

Edible gold metallic paint (optional)

1. Using hot pink line icing, pipe the outline of the bird. Pipe all around the outer edge of the biscuit, then add scalloped lines for the neck and wing and a curved line to define the chest. Leave to dry for 10 minutes at room temperature.
2. Once dry, flood the head and back wing sections of the bird with hot pink flood icing.
3. Flood the body of the bird with baby pink flood icing and the chest with white flood icing.
4. Place the biscuit onto a baking tray and into an oven set to the lowest temperature (50°C/gas mark ¼) for 40 minutes, or until the icing has set hard.
5. Use black line icing to pipe the eyes, beak and feet.
6. Use hot pink line icing to define the tail and wing feathers, piping a pattern of petal shapes over the baby pink area. On the hot pink wing, pipe baby pink petal shapes to create more feathers.
7. Add further detail with white line icing dots at the end of the feathers. If wished, you can alternate between white icing dots and edible gold metallic paint dots, applied with a clean dry paintbrush. Allow to fully dry.
8. You can also try icing these in reverse colours!

Sports Day Medals

Has sports fever taken over your household? If you're overrun by mini Mo Farahs, then this project is the perfect thing to keep them happy for an afternoon. Remember to buy some ribbon to thread through the biscuit – the medal ceremony is the best part!

You will need:

1 batch of circular biscuits* (recipes pp.19–25)

1 batch of white Royal Icing (recipe p.30), divided into line and flood consistencies

Clean paintbrushes or an airbrush

Edible metallic paints in gold, silver and bronze

Ribbon

* Don't forget to cut a generous hole towards the top of the biscuits, before baking, so you can thread your ribbons through later. Use the end of a drinking straw to cut out the perfect-sized hole from your uncooked dough!

1. Outline the shape of a circle on the biscuits in white line icing, followed by a small circle around the hole in the biscuit. Leave to dry for 10 minutes at room temperature.

2. Once dry, flood the biscuits with white flood icing.

3. Place the biscuits onto a baking tray and into an oven set to the lowest temperature (50°C/gas mark ¼) for 40 minutes, or until the icing has set hard.

4. Dip a clean paintbrush into the edible metallic paint and paint onto the biscuits. If you are making a big batch of these biscuits, you can also use an airbrush, if you have one. Leave the metallic paint to dry for 10 minutes.

5. Finally, ice on your numbers with white line icing and pipe the circle around the edge of the biscuit. Again, leave your biscuits to fully dry.

6. Thread through your ribbon and tie in a knot at the end.

School

Our school collection is the A* way to keep your revision hero motivated or to thank your hard-working teacher at the end of term. Learn how to write with icing on p.38 and personalise their very own school-bag biscuit for extra credit.

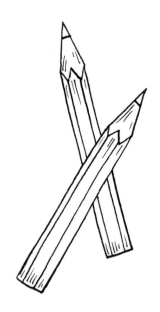

You will need:

1 batch of shaped biscuits (recipes pp.19–25)

1 batch of Royal Icing (recipe p.30), divided into line and flood consistencies (colours detailed in individual biscuit instructions)

Blackboard

Line: black / white
Flood: black

1. Use black line icing to pipe the rectangular outline of your blackboard on the biscuit. Leave to dry at room temperature for 10 minutes.

2. Once dry, flood the shape with black flood icing.

3. Place the biscuit onto a baking tray and into an oven set to the lowest temperature (50°C/gas mark ¼) for 40 minutes, or until the icing has set hard.

4. Use white line icing to ice a personal message onto the board or a funny joke to your favourite teacher! Allow to fully dry.

Satchel

Line: blue
Flood: blue / grey

1. Use blue line icing to outline a rectangular satchel shape on the biscuit. Leave to dry at room temperature for 10 minutes.

2. Once dry, fill the shape with blue flood icing.

3. Place the biscuit onto a baking tray and into an oven set to the lowest temperature (50°C/gas mark ¼) for 40 minutes, or until the icing has set hard.

4. Use blue line icing to ice on the details of the flap, straps, pocket and stitching and grey line icing for buckles and studs. Allow to fully dry.

School bus

Line: yellow / black / grey
Flood: yellow / black / white

1. Using yellow line icing, outline the shape of the bus on your biscuit, piping the main body of the bus, the mirrors, windows, destination sign and headlights.

2. Outline 2 round-cornered rectangles underneath the bus shape with black line icing – these will be the tyres. Leave to dry at room temperature for 10 minutes.

3. Once dry, flood the bus with yellow flood icing, the tyres with black flood icing and the destination sign and headlights with white flood icing.

4. Place the biscuit onto a baking tray and into an oven set to the lowest temperature (50°C/gas mark ¼) for 40 minutes, or until the icing has set hard.

5. Use black line icing to pipe round the destination sign and add any text if you wish, to define the front of the bus and the lines of the grate.

6. Finally, use grey line icing to add in the mirrors, detail to the tyres and a dot at the front of the bus. Allow to dry.

Jewish Celebrations

Celebrating their bar mitzvah or bat mitzvah is an important milestone in every Jewish teenager's life and this celebration of coming of age is marked by a fantastic party for family and friends. Our bat mitzvah and bar mitzvah collections make unique favours for guests to take home or a thoughtful thank-you gift for the hosts.

You will need:

1 batch of shaped biscuits (recipes pp.19–25)

1 batch of Royal Icing (recipe p.30), divided into line and flood consistencies (colours detailed in individual biscuit instructions)

Star of David

Line: white / pink / white
Flood: white

1. Use white line icing to outline the star shape on the biscuit. Leave to dry for 10 minutes at room temperature.

2. Once dry, flood the shape with white flood icing.

3. Place the biscuit onto a baking tray and into an oven set to the lowest temperature (50°C/gas mark ¼) for 40 minutes, or until the icing has set hard.

4. Use pink line icing to pipe the outline of the Star of David. You do this by piping a triangle, and then an upside-down triangle over the top. Allow to fully dry.

Kippah

Line: blue / beige / white
Flood: blue

1. Use blue line icing to pipe the outline of a kippah on an oval-shaped biscuit. Leave to dry for 10 minutes at room temperature.

2. Once dry, flood the shape with blue flood icing.

3. Place the biscuit onto a baking tray and into an oven set to the lowest temperature (50°C/gas mark ¼) for 40 minutes, or until the icing has set hard.

4. Using blue line icing, pipe 2 curved lines crossing over each other for the seams, then, across the bottom of the biscuit, pipe a row of small triangles with beige line icing. Directly above, pipe a row of downward-facing triangles with white line icing.

5. Finish off your biscuit by piping a Star of David in beige line icing at the top. Allow to fully dry.

Present

Line: baby pink / baby blue / white
Flood: baby pink

1. Using baby pink line icing, pipe the outline of the present on the biscuit. Leave to dry for 10 minutes at room temperature.

2. Once dry, flood the shape with baby pink flood icing.

3. Place the biscuit onto a baking tray and into an oven set to the lowest temperature (50°C/gas mark ¼) for 40 minutes, or until the icing has set hard.

4. Use baby blue line icing to pipe lots of dots over the present.

5. Finish by piping a line of white line icing down the centre of the biscuit and a bow at the top. Allow to fully dry.

Candle Biscuit Birthday Cake

This is one of our favourite cakes to make – the biscuit pop candles add an element of surprise and the icing isn't too complex.

You will need:

3 x 20-cm/8-inch Super Chocolatey Cake layers (recipe p.26)

1 batch of Chocolate Buttercream (recipe p.35)

25-cm/10-inch cake board

Icing sugar, for dusting

700g blue fondant icing (shop-bought, room temperature)

1 batch Royal Icing (recipe p.30), in colours of your choice

Biscuit Pop Candles (see instructions opposite)

1. Bake your cakes according to the recipe. Once the layers are completely cool, you can stack them up. Using a sharp knife, carefully level the top of each layer so they sit flat.

2. Smear a little buttercream onto the cake board and place the first cake layer on top, to secure it to the board.

3. Using a palette knife, spread buttercream evenly over the first layer and place another layer on top. Repeat.

4. Take a generous amount of buttercream and smooth it around the edge and top of the cake, using a palette knife or plastic side scraper to scrape off the excess, until the cake is evenly covered in buttercream.

5. Place the iced cake in the fridge for 30 minutes to firm up.

6. Measure across the top and sides of your cake using a piece of string or cotton – this will act as a guide for rolling out your fondant icing. Cut to size and set aside.

7. Clear a large, smooth work surface so that it is clean and free of crumbs – any imperfections will be visible on your fondant. Dust the surface generously with icing sugar.

8. Knead the fondant for 2 minutes, or until softened, then roll it into a ball and flatten into a disc shape.

9. Lightly dust a rolling pin with icing sugar. Roll out the fondant until it is about 5mm thick, giving it a quarter turn every now and then, to help keep it even and round. Use your measured string for guidance – the fondant should be slightly bigger than the string. You can always trim off excess fondant later.

10. Loosely drape the fondant over your rolling pin, then lift it and roll it up and over the cake.

11. Smooth the fondant over the cake with a fondant smoother or a smooth glass. Start on the top of the cake and then smooth down the sides. Be careful to avoid folds, wrinkles and air bubbles in the icing.

12. Once the fondant is smooth, use a small knife or pizza cutter to cut away any excess at the bottom of the cake. Try to cut as close to the bottom of the cake as possible.

13. Using lots of colourful line icing, pipe a design of balloons, presents and bunting directly onto the side of the cake. Allow to dry, then insert your biscuit pop candles into the cake.

Biscuit Pop Candles

1 batch of biscuit dough (recipes pp.19–25)

1 batch of Royal Icing (recipe p.30), divided into line and flood consistencies in the following colours:

Line: hot pink / yellow
Flood: hot pink / white

1. Roll out the dough to 7mm and cut into rectangular shapes with pointed tops. Before the biscuits are put in the oven to bake, carefully push wooden skewers into the length of the rectangle (see pp.15–16 for baking instructions and p.47 for biscuit pop tips).

2. Once the biscuits are baked and cooled, use hot pink line icing to outline rectangles on the biscuits, leaving space at the top for a flame. Leave to dry for 10 minutes at room temperature.

3. Once dry, alternate between hot pink and white flood icing to pipe diagonal stripes to fill the candle shapes.

4. Use yellow line icing to pipe flames on the tops.

5. Place the biscuits onto a baking tray and into an oven set to the lowest temperature (50°C/gas mark ¼) for 40 minutes, or until the icing has set hard.

6. Finally, if necessary, trim the end of your biscuit pop sticks.

Birthday Party Drink Toppers

Take your party to the next level with our biscuit drink toppers! Serve with milkshakes at a children's birthday party or with your favourite cocktail for a grown-up bash. Once your toppers are iced and completely dry and your cocktail recipe is mixed up and ready to go, assemble your drinks by sliding the biscuits onto straws and resting them on the edges of your bottles or glasses.

You will need:

1 batch of shaped biscuits* (recipes pp.19–25)

1 batch of Royal Icing (recipe p.30), divided into line and flood consistencies (colours detailed in individual biscuit instructions)

Colourful sprinkle decorations (for the Cupcake toppers)

* When cutting your biscuit dough, remember to cut a hole in the centre of your shapes for the straws, before baking. To do this, use something slightly bigger than a straw, such as a pen lid.

Cupcake toppers

Line: green / white / yellow
Flood: green / white

1. Use green line icing to pipe around the base of your biscuit to create the cupcake case. Outline the bottom half of the cut-out circle with the green line icing.

2. Pipe the outline of the cupcake frosting and the top of the cut-out circle with white line icing. Leave to dry for 10 minutes at room temperature.

3. Once dry, flood the cupcake case with green flood icing and the frosting section with white flood icing.

4. Place the biscuit onto a baking tray and into an oven set to the lowest temperature (50°C/gas mark ¼) for 40 minutes, or until the icing has set hard.

5. Pipe 2 thick lines across the frosting section with white line icing.

6. While the icing is still wet, sprinkle on some colourful sprinkle decorations and gently tap off any excess.

7. Finish with 5 vertical lines of yellow line icing on the cupcake case. Allow to fully dry.

Party ring toppers

Line: hot pink / yellow
Flood: hot pink

1. Using hot pink line icing, pipe a circle around the edge of a round biscuit and outline the central cut-out circle. Leave to dry for 10 minutes at room temperature.

2. Once dry, flood the ring with hot pink flood icing.

3. While the flood icing is still wet, use yellow line icing to pipe 4 horizontal lines across the biscuit.

4. Use a cocktail stick to vertically drag through the yellow lines in a single movement. Do this 3 times, in alternate directions. Wipe the cocktail stick clean between each drag.

5. Place the biscuit onto a baking tray and into an oven set to the lowest temperature (50°C/gas mark ¼) for 40 minutes, or until the icing has set hard.

Party Bag Jollies

Have you ever seen such a jolly line-up? Our family of gingers can be iced in a host of characters, which makes them very useful to have up your sleeve for party bags or the end of term.

You will need:

1 batch of shaped All-Spice Biscuits (recipe p.20)

1 batch of Royal Icing (recipe p.30), divided into line and flood consistencies (colours detailed in individual biscuit instructions)

Granulated sugar (for the Fairy princess)

Ballerina and Fairy princess

Line: brown / baby pink / white

1. Use brown line icing to pipe eyes and a smiley mouth onto the biscuit.
2. Continuing with brown icing, pipe the hair, then pipe the arms – you want the hands to touch in the middle.
3. Using baby pink or white line icing, pipe on a leotard, tutu and ballet shoes, and a wand for the fairy (don't pipe the tip immediately).
4. Use white or baby pink line icing to pipe on a hairband for the ballerina, or a crown and a star tip for the wand for the fairy princess. While the icing for the princess' crown and wand is still wet, sprinkle some sugar on top to make them sparkle! Tap off any excess and leave to fully dry.

Clown

Line: brown / red / white / yellow / green / orange

1. Pipe eyes and a smiley mouth with brown line icing. Pipe a medium-sized dot for his nose in red ling icing, then outline his mouth with white line icing.

2. Give your clown a funny hat – we've used yellow line icing for ours and then piped a small flower with green and white line icing.
3. Use white line icing to pipe his hands.
4. Using red and yellow line icing, pipe your clown some dungarees and a top. We've used a vertical stripy pattern for our clown's dungarees. Add buttons to his top in orange.
5. Finally, use green line icing to pipe his shoes and bowtie. Leave to fully dry.

Artist

Line: brown / black / red / blue / white / green

1. Pipe eyes and a smiley mouth with brown line icing. Pipe a beret in black ling icing, then strands of hair and a plait coming down on one side in brown line icing. Finish with a small line of red icing to look like a hair tie.
2. Outline the artist's smock with blue line icing, adding detail with 2 pockets at the waist.
3. Pipe the artist's hand with brown line icing, and a black line with a white drop at the top to look like a paintbrush. Add a dot of green icing to the tip of the brush.
4. Where the other hand would be, use white line icing to outline and fill in a small paint palette.
5. Finally, use blue, red and green line icing to add splodges of paint to the smock and palette. Leave to fully dry.

Gift Tags

Being a Biscuiteer is all about making special occasions more memorable. Our biscuit gift tags will transform even the dullest pair of socks into the most thoughtful present, not to mention giving them something delicious to dunk into their birthday morning cuppa.

You will need:

1 batch of shaped biscuits* (recipes pp.19–25)
1 batch of Royal Icing (recipe p.30), divided into line and flood consistencies, in colours of your choice

Line: colours of choice | black

Flood: white | colours of choice

* Don't forget to cut a generous hole towards the top of the biscuits, before baking, so you can thread your string/ribbons through later. Use the end of a drinking straw to cut out the perfect-sized hole from your uncooked dough!

1. Using a line icing colour of your choice, pipe the outline of your gift tag biscuit – don't forget to pipe around the small hole too.

2. In the centre of the biscuit pipe a large square or rectangle. Leave to dry for 10 minutes at room temperature.

3. When dry, flood the central area with white flood icing – be careful not to over-fill!

4. Flood the rest of the biscuit with the same colour flood icing as the line icing.

5. Place the biscuits onto a baking tray and into an oven set to the lowest temperature (50°C/gas mark ¼) for 40 minutes, or until the icing has set hard.

6. Pipe around the outline of the central white area with the same coloured line icing you used earlier.

7. In a contrasting colour of line icing, pipe your decorative detail. We piped dots, swirls and stars.

8. Finally, use black line icing to pipe the recipient's name or a personal gift message onto the central white area. Allow to fully dry.

9. Take a length of thin ribbon or string and thread it through the small hole in your biscuits, tying it in a knot to secure.

Wedding Favours

Master these traditional designs and you'll be set for every friend's wedding, hen party or engagement. We often ice big batches for our customers' wedding favours, with bespoke colours to match the bride and groom's big day. For inspiration on packaging wedding favours, check out our gift-wrapping ideas on p.42.

You will need:

1 batch of shaped biscuits (recipes pp.19–25)

1 batch of Royal Icing (recipe p.30), divided into line and flood consistencies (colours detailed in individual biscuit instructions)

Silver ball decorations (for the Wedding bell)

Bouquet

Line: dark green / light green / light pink / purple / white

1. Use dark green line icing to pipe a tight starburst shape on your biscuit. Then pipe 3 lines at different lengths for the stalks. Leave to dry for 10 minutes at room temperature.

2. Over the top, ice a smaller starburst shape with light green line icing and then add 3 lines for additional stalks. Leave to dry for 10 minutes.

3. Use light pink line icing to pipe some flowers and then pipe flowers in the gaps with purple line icing.

4. Pipe a scattering of dots with white line icing and then add a white bow to the stems to finish. Allow to fully dry.

Wedding bell

Line: white
Flood: white

1. Using white line icing, outline the shape of the bell on your biscuit. Leave to dry for 10 minutes at room temperature.

2. Once dry, use white flood icing to fill in the shape, but don't over-fill.

3. Place the biscuit onto a baking tray and into an oven set to the lowest temperature (50°C/gas mark ¼) for 40 minutes, or until the icing has set hard.

4. Use white line icing to pipe a bow across the bell, and then pipe a large dot at the bottom of the bell.

5. While the icing is still wet, gently press a silver ball decoration onto the dot of icing at the bottom. Allow to fully dry.

Wedding dress

Line: white
Flood: white

1. Using white line icing, pipe the outline of the dress on your biscuit. Leave to dry for 10 minutes at room temperature.

2. Once dry, use white flood icing to fill in the shape, but don't over-fill.

3. Place the biscuit onto a baking tray and into an oven set to the lowest temperature (50°C/gas mark ¼) for 40 minutes, or until the icing has set hard.

4. Use white line icing to pipe two long 'fold' lines down the dress and to add extra detail to the bust of the dress. Add lacey details, outlining the neck and sleeves and then filling in with piped squiggles. Allow to fully dry.

Wedding Place Settings

These personalised biscuits act as both place settings and favours for your wedding guests. Be as creative as you like with the biscuit design, the most memorable weddings are full of unique touches that are personal to the happy couple. We've iced lots of wedding dress replicas and even football strips!

You will need:

1 batch of shaped biscuits (recipes pp.19–25)

1 batch of Royal Icing (recipe p.30), divided into line and flood consistencies (colours detailed in individual biscuit instructions)

Car

Line: white / grey / baby pink / green / black
Flood: white / grey

1. Ice the outline of the car in white line icing on your biscuit. Then outline the window and tyres in grey line icing. Leave to dry for 10 minutes at room temperature.

2. Once dry, fill in the car shape with white flood icing, then fill in the window and car tyres with grey flood icing.

3. Place the biscuit onto a baking tray and into an oven set to the lowest temperature (50°C/gas mark ¼) for 40 minutes, or until the icing has set hard.

4. Outline the window with white line icing, then pipe a rectangle underneath – this is where the guest's name goes. Add baby pink line icing bow streamers and little polka dots of green. Use grey line icing to pipe the back headlights.

5. Ice your writing into the rectangular box using black line icing (see p.38 for advice on this technique). Allow to fully dry.

Heart

Line: white / light pink / light green / black
Flood: white

1. Pipe the outline of a heart on your biscuit with white line icing. Leave to dry for 10 minutes at room temperature.

2. Once dry, flood the shape with white flood icing.

3. Place the biscuit onto a baking tray and into an oven set to the lowest temperature (50°C/gas mark ¼) for 40 minutes, or until the icing has set hard.

4. Pipe a ruffled frame around the edge of the biscuit in light pink line icing.

5. In each corner of the biscuit pipe 3 small leaf shapes with light green line icing. Then pipe little swirls on top in light pink line icing.

6. Add your guest's name to the middle of the biscuit in black line icing. Allow to fully dry.

Wedding cake

Line: white / light pink / black
Flood: white

1. Outline all 3 tiers of the cake and the heart at the top in white line icing. Leave to dry for 10 minutes at room temperature.

2. Once dry, flood with white flood icing.

3. Place the biscuit onto a baking tray and into an oven set to the lowest temperature (50°C/gas mark ¼) for 40 minutes, or until the icing has set hard.

4. Pipe lines with light pink line icing at the top of each cake tier.

5. With white line icing, add ribbons and bows to the tiers and connect them together with lines.

6. Add your guest's name at the top of the biscuit in black line icing. Allow to fully dry.

Specialist suppliers of cutters, sprinkles and equipment

Cakes, Cookies & Crafts:

cakescookiesandcraftsshop.co.uk

More cutters than you could possibly imagine,
as well as specialist ingredients, such as Meri-White
powdered egg white, decorations and bakeware.

Squires Kitchen:

squires-shop.com

The place to go for all things biscuit! Icing,
colouring, edible paint, colours – you name it!

The Craft Company:

craftcompany.co.uk

Everything you need for making biscuits and cakes.

The Cake Craft Shop:

cakecraftshop.co.uk

For all your biscuit needs!

Lakeland:

lakeland.co.uk

Good for all things baking.

Blends Limited:

blendsltd.co.uk

For all flavourings and colourings.

Divertimenti:

divertimenti.co.uk

Specialist and professional bakeware
and equipment.

Amazon:

amazon.co.uk

There isn't a biscuit cutter, colour or shimmer
you can't find on Amazon!

General Ingredients:

Waitrose:

waitrose.com

Lots of good-quality baking ingredients.

Ocado:

ocado.com

Home delivery for all ingredients and baking essentials.

Tesco:

tesco.com

Lots of baking ingredients and icing essentials.

Sainsbury's:

sainsburys.co.uk

Lots of baking ingredients and icing essentials.

Index

Illustrations are in bold.

This book is the result of lots of hard work by the whole team at Biscuiteers and includes some of our favourite projects that have been created by a group of very talented people.

Extra-special thanks to:

The incredible Victoria Sawdon: book designer and Biscuiteers illustrator.

Cassie Merrick, Bryony Lockhart and Daisy Kent, our brilliant copy writers.

Bryony Lockhart, organisational superstar, who made everything happen.

Our wonderful biscuit designers, Lucy Simmons and Julia Chung, who iced all of the biscuits in this book.

Our talented pastry chef, Mark Hammerton, who made all of the cakes.

The bakery team, headed up by Rachel Cullen; the icing team, headed up by Margarida Andrade; and the rest of our inspiring colleagues at Biscuiteers HQ.

Katie Hammond, our super-creative photographer; Matt Walder, our photography assistant; and Emily Mayor, our prop stylist.

Emily Preece-Morrison, our copy editor.

Ione Walder, our commissioning editor at Penguin, and Clare Hulton, our agent, who have helped us create a book we are truly proud of.

And, most importantly, we would like to thank our wonderful customers, who are creating a world of thoughtful gifters, one biscuit at a time.

MICHAEL JOSEPH

UK | USA | Canada | Ireland | Australia
India | New Zealand | South Africa

Michael Joseph is part of the Penguin Random House
group of companies whose addresses can be found
at global.penguinrandomhouse.com.

Penguin
Random House
UK

First published by Michael Joseph, 2018
001

Text copyright © Harriet Hastings, 2018
Photography © Katie Hammond, 2018
Except for p.10 (centre-right image) © Selfridges
Illustrations © Victoria Sawdon, 2018
Design and layout by Victoria Sawdon at Big Fish
Edited by Emily Preece-Morrison
Styling by Emily Mayor
The moral right of the author and illustrator has been asserted

Printed in China

Colour reproduction by Alta

A CIP catalogue record for this book is available from the British Library
ISBN: 978-0-718-18859-7

www.greenpenguin.co.uk

MIX
Paper from
responsible sources
FSC® C018179

Penguin Random House is committed to a
sustainable future for our business, our readers
and our planet. This book is made from Forest
Stewardship Council® certified paper.